Inclinations

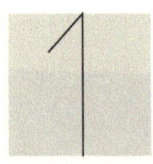

SQUARE ONE
First-Order Questions in the Humanities

PAUL A. KOTTMAN, Series Editor

INCLINATIONS

A Critique of Rectitude

Adriana Cavarero
Translated by Amanda Minervini and Adam Sitze

STANFORD UNIVERSITY PRESS
STANFORD, CALIFORNIA

Stanford University Press
Stanford, California

Inclinations: A Critique of Rectitude was originally published in Italian under the title *Inclinazioni: Critica della rettitudine* © 2014, Rafaello Cortina Editore.

This book has been published with the support of the Department of Philosophy, Education, and Psychology, University of Verona.

Library of Congress Cataloging-in-Publication Data is available from the Library of Congress

ISBN 9780804792189 (cloth : alk. paper)
ISBN 9781503600409 (pbk. : alk. paper)
ISBN 9781503600416 (electronic)

Cover art: Leonardo da Vinci, *The Virgin and Child with St. Anne*. Wikimedia Commons
Cover design: Rob Ehle

Text design: Bruce Lundquist
Typeset at Stanford University Press in 10/14 Minion Pro

Contents

Foreword
Paul A. Kottman

Adriana Cavarero's *Inclinations* is not just a "correction" of rectitude, but a *critique of rectitude*. That is, this book investigates the discursive conditions of possibility for the characterization of the human being as upright, erect. Cavarero proposes *inclination* not simply as the "real" nature of the human being, by unmasking uprightness as a wrong characterization of our true essence. Instead, Cavarero investigates the way in which human beings have been *figured* or depicted as upright, in philosophy, psychoanalysis, anthropological writings, literature and artworks.

Cavarero aims to shed light, in particular, on the *effects* of this figuration, the "truths" and "power relations" that these discursive or artistic figurations produce and install. Given the long-standing depiction of human (in particular, male) uprightness and rectitude, it seems less fruitful to ask whether these figurations were "correct" depictions of human beings. (An emphasis on "correctness" could itself be seen as one of the effects under investigation.) Cavarero is interested, rather, in tallying the costs of depicting the human being as upright when it comes to our view of women, our overall understanding and collective self-conception.

One effect of the figuration of the human being as "upright," Cavarero suggests, has been to obscure another, perhaps more natural, figuration for people in their relation to one another: inclination. Cavarero returns to themes she has discussed thoughtfully in other writings over the course of her career: maternity, love, representations of women. She "distills," as she puts it, a "rhetoric of inclination," in order to superimpose it "like a transparent screen, over the rhetoric of the philosophical subject, to highlight the differences between the two ontological, ethical, and political models."

For Cavarero, artworks, literary texts, and philosophical discourses are not just passive "reflections" of social realities. Nor do art and philosophy simply mirror the prejudices or belief systems of a historical era—such as patriarchy, or Christian morality. Instead, she treats art and philosophy as a matrix for the understanding of our cultural heritage. Cavarero interprets philosophical texts and artworks in order to see *how* human lives and interactions have been understood—and, thus, how they might be understood differently. It is in this sense that Cavarero's work is concerned with first-order questions in the humanities.

At a certain point in *Inclinations*, for instance, Cavarero interprets the significance of Leonardo da Vinci's depiction of Mary in his painting *The Virgin and Child with St. Anne*. She contrasts Mary's inclined body and outstretched arms, in the Leonardo painting, to the immobility of the Byzantine Theotokos, which presents the upright Christ figure to the viewer. Although Cavarero does not mention Hegel in this regard, I could not help but recall the way in which Hegel, too—in his *Lectures on Fine Art*—saw in Italian painting an emancipation from the understanding of human beings presented in late Byzantine icons. Like Cavarero, Hegel even singles out Leonardo for praise in this regard. Hegel, moreover, agrees with Cavarero regarding the world-historical significance of these painterly depictions of maternity and maternal love, which expand our understanding of what it is to be human. In Cavarero's hands, artworks and philosophical texts shed light on our fundamental self-conceptions—as mothers, children, lovers—and how these change over time.

Inclinations

Introduction

> *Inclination* is not a steady state; it is a
> slope, as the word says, a disposition
> toward affect, which comes from certain
> likable qualities in the object: but it may
> become affect or impetuous love.
>
> Niccolò Tommaseo, *Nuovo dizionario*
> *dei sinonimi della lingua italiana*

IN A FRAGMENT on the concept of *inclination* in Kant, the young
Walter Benjamin wrote that a change of perspective on the meaning
of the term could turn it into one of the most fundamental concepts of
morality.[1] Because of the fragment's brevity, it is not clear what Benjamin means. It is plausible that he meant to criticize the negative mode
in which the ethical tradition regards human inclinations, pledging
to provide a means adequate for their containment or control. Kant,
therefore, is perhaps only a pretext—or better, the exemplary case of
a general philosophical attitude that, relative to a positive revaluation
of inclination, is not cause for optimism. Whatever Benjamin had in
mind, his fragment fell on hostile ground. Philosophy, in general, does
not appreciate inclination; it contests and combats it. Its methods are
numerous and varied, depending on the epoch, but are all, in essence,
as Foucault would put it, *dispositifs* of verticalization the aim of which

is the upright man [*l'uomo retto*].[2] And already, on the linguistic plane, this provides a clear indication of the geometrical structure underlying the question.

Of course, geometers and scientists have an excellent rapport with the concept of inclination. In their vocabulary, the term simply indicates "a divergent position or direction from the horizontal line," which is to say a declivity, or a "divergent position or direction from the vertical line," which is to say, a slope.[3] The picture is clear, precise, formalized, and in this field, the term does not create problems; to the contrary, it allows for the analysis and resolution of problems. Nor does it create hostility; any emotional tone is programmatically absent. The same cannot be said about the many philosophers and other experts who, in various ways and with uncertain results, have for centuries discussed the thorny problem of human inclinations. Here, indeed, nothing is clear: geometrical exactitude suddenly vanishes and the greatest disquietude reigns. According to modern dictionaries, when the term moves from geometry to common speech and, even more, to philosophical language, it makes a crucial leap, from its proper sense to a figurative sense—which, as usually happens, inevitably complicates the situation. Philosophy, for its part, together with theology, often surrounds the term with fateful adjectives, making the question of its meaning even more difficult. In moral treatises, for instance, it is easy to encounter a conflict between "good inclination," which is to say "an innate or acquired disposition to act virtuously," and its opposite, "bad inclination," a "natural and acquired propensity to behave dishonestly," which is to say, in a depraved manner. Then there is the fact that philosophical language tends to include under the general definition of inclination the vast and frightening catalog of desires, instincts, and passions. Indeed, in a speculative vocabulary, "inclination" and "passion" are used often as synonyms. The theme of love is proof enough: as Kant writes, "The one who loves another wishes him well, but without owing it to him; he acts, rather, from a willing disposition, gladly, and from his own impulse. Love is well-wishing from inclination."[4] And Kant, in turn, worries that love may transform itself, inexorably, into appetite.

Sexual and emotional inclination toward a person—for brevity's sake, we'll call it eros—stirs serious apprehension, above all among philosophers. They perceive it as a threat to the subject's equilibrium—a deep quiver, a slippery slope. With his famous theory of the erotic way to philosophy, Plato might be an exception. But we shouldn't forget that even he casts aspersions on another type of inclination, namely, artistic inclination, or, more precisely, the inclination of those who lean (*apoklinei*) toward "technics."[5] This is a good place to highlight the etymological root of the term *inclination*, which already has started coming into view: to incline is to bend, to lean down, to lower; in Greek, *klinè* means "bed." Traditionally, however, it is not artistic inclination that most worries the philosophers. What they fear most of all are inclinations that are too impetuous and difficult to master. In the turbulent realm of eros, these include the inclination that turns to lust and other pleasures of the flesh—prominent among which is the alleged propensity of specifically female nature to lasciviousness. In traditional ethics, this argument is often developed with particular passion, but it also appears in authors who would seem to be more open-minded. In the mid-nineteenth century, for example, the influential philosopher Pierre Proudhon, known for his innovative and revolutionary ideas, wrote some passages on this theme that are worthy of mention. "To speak of sexual relations, it is a law of nature in all animals that the female, incited by the instinct to have children, searches for a male in all manner of ways. Woman cannot escape this law. She is naturally more inclined to lasciviousness than man, first because her self is more fragile, such that liberty and intelligence struggle in her with less force against her animalistic inclinations, and secondly because love is the great, if not only, occupation of her life."[6]

Despite his misogyny, or perhaps precisely because his prejudice does not spare even maternity, Proudhon's words are ultimately thought-provoking. Following a widely accepted theory, Proudhon argues that love, with its pathologies and excesses, is essentially rooted in natural and animal phenomena related to sexual inclination, understood not as an orientation for a particular sex but as the instinct to have sex. He also suggests that, in women as in females of other species, this instinct is subordinated to the instinct for procreation. From this perspective, erotic and maternal inclinations spring from a core that is as imperious and indomitable as nature itself. Obviously, were woman a free and rational individual, she too, like the male of the human species, would be able to oppose the rule of the instincts. But because nature instead provided her with a rather weak ego, "liberty and intelligence struggle in her with less force against her animalistic inclinations." For Proudhon, in short, the weak sex represents a reality in which inclinations rage out of control, and are therefore stronger and more dangerous; the fact that pleasures of the flesh (perhaps sugar-coated with romantic ideals) are closely associated with maternal inclination makes the issue even more disquieting. For Schopenhauer too—to remain within nineteenth-century philosophy—feminine nature is characterized by a perfect short-circuit between lasciviousness, giving birth, and the instinctual care of offspring. After condemning the indecent female art of seduction, he writes that "women in truth exist entirely for the propagation of the race, and their destiny ends here." He adds that although women are suited for the care of children, "they themselves are childish, foolish, and short-sighted—in a word, they are big children all their lives, something intermediate between the child and the man, who is a man in the strict sense of the word."[7] One may find this passage excessively misogynist; in essence, however, it has a broad consensus within a respected tradition: in the library of the West, whenever discussion turns to the dangers of inclinations, women are regularly in the mix. From this perspective, the well-known theological doctrine on original sin that ascribes an innate *inclinatio ad malum* to the whole human race appears less sexist. If everyone is inclined toward evil, the starting point is, however dismaying, nevertheless equal regardless of gender.

With the thesis of a congenital and originary inclination to evil, we face an extreme, perhaps totalizing, case that resoundingly escapes established critical frameworks. Philosophy, as a rule, avoids bringing the whole system of human inclinations back to a single, predestined origin. It instead limits itself to denunciations of the more or less devastating effect of some inclinations, above all those related to the sexual sphere, and often it does not even try to offer a complete map. Although characterized by certain constants, this framework is essentially open to numerous variants: in different epochs and contexts, certain inclinations—at times considered natural, at times socially acquired, or the result of a perversion—are more worrisome than others. Compared to a precise recognition of the problem, this is of course still too general, but it at least provides an opportunity to point out another fact regularly registered in dictionaries. Not all the phenomena that language ascribes to the term *inclination* interest philosophers; indeed, many possible meanings remain consistently marginal to speculative turbulence and receive little attention from philosophers. Whereas the discourse of the moral tradition surrounds the concept of inclination with alarm, ordinary language—which philosophers can also rely upon—allows it to be used in an innocuous or even banal way, indeed, without frightening anyone. There is here, it would seem, a vast no-man's land, indifferent or neutral, or, at least, not immediately worrisome for moral discipline and, hence, irrelevant. This no-man's land includes the inclinations that define a temperament or character, such as the inclination to melancholy or to solitude, to happiness or to optimism, and many more. It also includes inclinations to a certain activity or form of amusement, to the range of activities that everyday vocabulary all too hastily calls hobbies. Those inclined to fishing or puzzles don't really alarm philosophers or moralists all that much; those inclined to meditation or reasoning, by contrast, arouse philosophers' appreciation. In its common sense—as a synonym for "propensity," "taste," "disposition," "predisposition," and "tendency"—the term is particularly flexible and easily shakes off the negative valences that appear in the domain of ethical reflection. It depends, precisely, on the context.

When the context is purely philosophical and pertains to Kant, things always seem to take an interesting turn. In addition to Benjamin, Hannah Arendt offers further proof in her 1965 lectures on Kant at the New School entitled "Some Questions of Moral Philosophy." In those lectures, Arendt did not miss the chance to underline that "every inclination turns outward, it leans out of the self in the direction of whatever may affect me from the outside world."[8] Despite its apparent simplicity, this utterance is worthy of much consideration. Not only does it have the merit of reminding us that the meaning of the word inclination points to a geometrical imaginary; it also, above all, clarifies that, in the theater of modern philosophy, center stage is occupied by an I whose position is straight and vertical.[9] Words like *righteousness* and *rectitude*, which occur frequently in dictionaries of morals, and were often used already in the Middle Ages for the "rectification" of bad inclinations, are an important anticipation of this scenario. The "upright man" of which the tradition speaks, more than an abused metaphor, is literally a subject who conforms to a vertical axis, which in turn functions as a principle and norm for its ethical posture. One can thus understand why philosophers see inclination as a perpetual source of apprehension, which is renewed in each epoch, and which takes on even more weight during modernity, when the free and autonomous self celebrated by Kant enters the scene. As we might say with Arendt, the thrust of inclination knocks the I from its internal center of gravity and, by making it lean to the outside, "be they objects or people,"[10] undermines its stability. Besides posing a moral problem for the modern conception of the self, inclination is a matter of structural equilibrium and thus, in the end, becomes an ontological question as well. An inclined I, leaning toward the outside, is no longer straight: it leans forward with respect to the vertical line that supports it and that, because it allows it to balance itself, makes it an autonomous and independent subject. For Kant, who is the most ardent supporter of perfect autonomy, this is a very serious outcome.

Even common people who may be unfamiliar with philosophy know that the most frequent and feared inclination, love, is an attack against the self's balance. To fall in love, to be moved outside of the self, to give in to the attraction coming from another person and to slide down a slope that pulls irresistibly—this is a big mess for everyone. To lean or depend on the other, to rely on the other rather than preserving one's own autonomy—this is the same kind of trouble, only now expressed philosophically, in strictly Kantian terms. Maria Zambrano observes that in love "the center of gravity of the person moves, first of all, to the loved person, and when love disappears, that movement 'outside of the self' remains, even though that position is difficult to maintain," because "to be a man means to be steady, to weigh on something,"[11] to rest perpendicularly on one's base. More than mystics, here it would be appropriate to let poets, or narrators, speak. Proust, for instance, uses illuminating metaphors when describing Swann's ruinous love for Odette in *Search for Lost Time*. Regarding the walk to his beloved's house, which Swann performs obsessively every evening, he writes: "the path that separated him from her was the one he inevitably traveled as though it were the slope itself, rapid and irresistible, of his life."[12] In the case of "falling in love" and other sweeping passions, inclination is not only a powerful force that pushes the self outside itself, but also an oblique plane on which the self slides without bannisters. The euphoria children feel playing on slides is testimony that, in abandoning oneself to the laws of gravity, in assenting to descent without resistance, there is an intrinsic pleasure. For his part, Proust writes, Swann felt that the inescapable slope of his love obeyed "immutable and natural laws" and that, in the rare moments when he seemed to recover his old balance, "little by little he became himself again, but possessed by another."[13] Inclination bends and dispossesses the I. As is often said, the attractions of love remove self-control from the I, causing it to get carried away and to exit itself: this, precisely, is the meaning of *ek-stasis*. Erotic inclination, accordingly, has an intrinsically ecstatic effect, even without the ultimate enjoyment that some, not surprisingly, call ecstasy.

Love overwhelms, dispossesses, and sometimes leads to a romantic death—the literature on this phenomenon is, as we know, immense. Men as well as women suffer it, but, as Proudhon and others believe, it especially afflicts women because of their structural absence of a stable self. Paradigmatic in this sense, to remain in the realm of masterpieces of the western novel, is the figure of Anna Karenina, in whom the devastating and exemplary lethal force of the inclination of love comes into conflict with maternal inclination. When it reveals its full power, it sweeps her away with its blind fury: "If I could be anything else but a mistress who passionately loves only his caresses—

but I cannot and do not want to be anything else," says the unfortunate woman in the delirious soliloquy preceding her suicide. Then,
when remembering the love she once felt for her son, she coherently
adds: "But I did live without him, exchanged him for another love,
and didn't complain of the exchange as long as I was satisfied by that
love."[14] Tolstoy already had warned the reader that if Count Vronsky
should say to Anna "resolutely, passionately, without a moment's hesitation: 'Abandon everything and fly away with me!'—she would leave
her son and go with him."[15] This is an easy prophecy, of course, for
the omniscient author, who does not hesitate to linger on the defini-
tive collapse of maternal inclination in the face of the passion of love,
narrating how Anna, after abandoning her legitimate child, is then
able to feel affection for the daughter—the love-child—she had with
her paramour. That in such a context eros easily can claim victory is
already clear from the conservative tradition which, since antiquity,
has assigned women two distinct social roles: while some women
are destined for the use of pleasure, others are supposed to dedicate
themselves to the domestic sphere and to maternal care. As an un-
faithful wife, and hence as a depraved woman—lost to herself and
to society—Anna Karenina overcomes precisely the limit that keeps
these two ambits distinct. In an open confrontation between maternal
inclination and inclination for her lover, once the barrier that should
have enclosed eros has fallen, the former ends up succumbing to the
latter. Certainly, the fight could have ended differently under different
skies and in different times; but the novel is emblematic precisely because of how the story unfolds, up to and including the final suicide.
The misogynistic vein, which pulses through Tolstoy's masterpiece,
needs the fallen woman to die, and she does so in a horrible way, even
more so because she is a mother.

Reduced to its bare plot, Anna Karenina's story is banal, didactic, and melodramatic, not unlike the story of another famous female character, Emma Bovary, whose treatment is even more pitiless.
Flaubert's novel reiterates an old and severe lesson: adulterous love,
forbidden to women and tolerated in men, cannot but transform bad
wives into bad mothers. In the great books of world literature as in

the feuilletons, which narrate the unequal relation between the arrows of eros and the married woman, a stereotypical view of the feminine predominates. This applies to many different aspects of the way that feminine character is dramatized, but it is especially true of the conventional image of maternal inclination. In order to emphasize the scandal of maternal inclination succumbing to eros, emphasis is placed on the traditional traits of the self-sacrificing mother who, absorbed by the care of her children, is completely fulfilled and sublimely happy. Not without a touch of sarcasm, Tolstoy has one of the novel's most libertine characters (one who, unlike Anna, will not be punished) define Anna Karenina as "*une couveuse*," a nesting female who incubates her "brood."[16] In English, one would say that she's a "mother hen." The basic idea, idyllically rural, is that a mother/hen reclining on a soft bed with her baby/chicks should be an effective metaphor for woman's natural inclination for the joys of maternity. But if it is true that the term inclination insists on a geometrical imaginary, then this picture ends up confounding established coordinates. The expected oblique line, which unbalances the self's vertical axis, making it lean toward the outside, is here replaced by an unusual horizontal line that rests tranquilly on the ground. In other words, and not without irony, the mother who reposes with her "brood" does not lean forward or toward her infant, as in Christian iconology pertaining to the Virgin Mary. She instead sits on her child, running the risk of smothering him. It is indeed a curious postural variant. The figure of the upright I standing in erect position, which already is denied to the "weak sex" by nature, here inclines so low that it becomes a squat—which, whatever else one may say about it, at least avoids the risk of slippage.

As the iconology of the Virgin Mary testifies, even though the mother is bent over the infant, tilting to the exterior, she doesn't slip. Leaning over the other, forming an oblique line, she reposes in tranquility, in a static and perfect equilibrium. Indeed, when the figure is that of the Madonna bent over baby Jesus, a figure popularized by religious art, she stays immobile and crystallized, in a "frozen state," as if maternal inclination were not a movement but an originary and natural mold, an archetypical posture. The effect of this crystallization is, in truth, remarkable: on the symbolic plane, it is also empowered by an image of maternity so pure that it excludes any interference by eros. Paradoxically, to the extent that she rises to the level of a moral example, the Virgin Mary "establishes the child as the destiny of woman, but escapes the sexual intercourse necessary for all other women to fulfill this destiny."[17] Also on account of this paradox, at least as compared to the postural geometry of ethics, and with reference to the true or presumed nature of the two sexes, the picture is, after all, simplified: avoiding the usual subordination of the feminine to the masculine, each sex ends up acquiring an originary posture because of its specific being. Next to the paradigm of the vertical axis, appropriated by man because of his inborn rationality, appears the paradigm of an oblique line, reserved to woman because of a constitutive predisposition to maternity, which causes inclination. It is of course indisputable that we are speaking here about outdated stereotypes: the schema works, precisely, by emphatically and repeatedly proposing conventional characteristics for the two sexes. But looking closer, and through a philosophical frame, we see two postural paradigms referring to two different models of subjectivity, two theaters for questioning the human condition in terms of autonomy or independence, two styles of thought, two languages: the first relates to individualistic ontology, the second to a relational ontology. Retracing the distinction between one outline that is masculine and another that is exquisitely feminine makes for a very interesting operation. In her famous book *The Second Sex* Simone de Beauvoir writes: "A man is in his right by virtue of being a man; it is the woman who is in the wrong. In fact, just as for the ancients there was an absolute vertical that defined the oblique, there is an absolute human type that is masculine."[18] Given that two sexes are in question here, the problem is not so much, or not only, to contest the absoluteness of the vertical axis, but also to free inclination from its normative command and its defining grip.

"THE METHOD OF EXAGGERATION, of the extremization [*die Extremisierung*] of every important and correct insight," is, according to Hans Jonas, a typical trait of Arendt's thought.[19] Even though this claim is not malevolent, it is perhaps the case that Jonas him-self is here exaggerating, pushing to the extreme his own judgment of Arendt. For those who have some familiarity with Arendt's texts, there is nevertheless something true in this judgment. In the follow-ing pages, through an emphatic forcing of maternal inclination, we will try to imitate Arendt's method—beginning with the idea, un-doubtedly important and correct, that Arendt introduces when she frames inclination in postural terms and relates it to the geometry of the subject. Among the various geometries of modernity, the prevail-ing one involves precisely the individualistic ontological model, which can be found in Kant. This model is widely known; later I will submit its egocentric verticality to a detailed deconstruction. Right now it will be more useful to refer briefly to its latest misadventures. Far from having a peaceful and undisputed reign, the autocratic, integrated and cohesive ego has been under attack for at least a century; in the twen-tieth century, it has been the main target of various critical currents that, in the wake of the postmodern wave, focus primarily on the frag-mentation of the subject. In fact, even today, despite the apparent de-cline of the postmodern, one must resist the temptation to break the subject down into fragments, turning its pretense of unity into a feast of difference. Instead of continuing to fragment the subject, one could try—drawing on Arendt—to incline it. Instead of breaking its vertical axis into multiple pieces, one could try bending it, giving it a different posture. This could perhaps happen by inclining the subject toward the *other*—as the relational model allows and, from a geometrical per-spective, even encourages.

Without any pretense of covering the topic exhaustively, I will use the expression *relational model* as a generic rubric to include the various theoretical perspectives that, in the panorama of philosophy today, concentrate on the category of *relation* to rethink a subjectiv-ity marked by exposure, vulnerability, and dependence. This trend is connected in many ways to the most recent products of feminist thought, in whose vocabulary one finds expressions such as "new em-bodied ontology," "ontology of the human," or "altruistic ethics," and whose more or less hidden aspiration—according to some—is a new "humanism."[20] In this theoretical field, Arendt's relational conception of the human and her political views are often openly invoked, sometimes in conjunction with the treatment of the theme of *vulnerability* developed in the writings of Emmanuel Lévinas. It is not by chance that both thinkers gained great attention by writing about the tragedy of totalitarian violence. A passage from Lévinas may prove useful to frame this question more clearly. In *Proper Names*, when commenting on the transition of twentieth-century philosophy from the individualistic to the relational model, he writes:

> The history of the theory of knowledge in contemporary philosophy is the history of the disappearance of the subject/object problem. Contemporary philosophy denounces as an abstraction the subject closed in upon itself and metaphysically the origin of itself and the world. The consistency of the self is dissolved into relations: intentionality in Husserl, being-in-the world or *Miteinandersein* in Heidegger, or continual renewal of *durée* in Bergson. Concrete reality is man always already in relation to the world, or always already projected beyond his instant. These relations cannot be reduced to theoretical representation. The latter would only confirm the autonomy of the thinking subject. In order to demolish the idea of the subject closed in upon itself, one must uncover, beneath objectification, very different relations that sustain it: man is in situation before situating himself.[21]

For Lévinas, demolishing the autonomous and closed subject to affirm an open and relational subjectivity isn't just an epistemological operation; it doesn't just refound ethics on the primacy of the *Other*. It aims, above all, at countering the violence of the egocentric subject. Precisely this aspect, considered vis-à-vis an eschatological vision of peace that "breaks the totality of wars and empires,"[22] makes Lévinas's thought especially interesting in the broad field of criticism that tries to redefine the relational model. The true target of this heterogeneous and varied field is not, in fact—or not only—the philosophical genealogy of the subject; it is the violent practices of domination, exclusion, and devastation of which the subject itself is an accomplice (ranging from racism to sexism, to homophobia, as well as war and other regular or irregular forms of destruction). The emphasis on vulnerability, in the relational model invoked here, is therefore first of all an accent on politics, ethics, and the social. The choice of assuming vulnerability as a paradigm of the human, far from an abstract speculative move, is instead rooted in the analysis of concrete situations and, as Judith Butler would say, of precarious lives that are especially exposed. As Butler herself observes: "It won't even do to say that I am promoting a relational view of the self over an autonomous one or trying to redescribe autonomy in terms of relationality."[23] That is to say: emphasizing vulnerability is not a matter of correcting individualistic ontology by inserting the category of relation into it. It is rather to think relation itself as originary and constitutive, as an essential dimension of the human, which—far from limiting itself to putting free and autonomous individuals in relation to each other, as the doctrine of the social pact prescribes—calls into question our being creatures who are materially vulnerable and, often in greatly unbalanced circumstances, consigned to one another.

In its radical version, which liquidates any residue of individualistic ontology, the relational model does not in fact allow for any symmetry at all, but only for a continuous interweaving of multiple and singular dependence. At its most extreme, it is exemplified by scenarios in which the protagonists are altogether unbalanced. Chief among these is the "primary scene," in which the infant finds itself in a condition of absolute and unilateral dependence on others, or more obviously, on the mother. But precisely this obviousness—and this is a crucial part of the problem, on which we must insist—instead of being used or perhaps recoded, destructured, and rethought, is often censured and silenced. Put differently: at the same time that the infant, as the emblem of a unilateral and absolute dependence, often appears at center stage to exemplify relational ontology, the mother, because of the burdensome self-sacrificing stereotype that is draped over her, is often absent. However understandable this absence may be in cultural terms, it nevertheless hinders philosophical speculation. That which, because of what seems by now to be an intractable stereotype, is lost to reflection is not just the ordinary and, if you will, banal experience of thousands of loving mothers bending over their child, but, above all, a popular imaginary that has the dubious merit, it would seem, of keeping the subject's posture under check. If the aim is finally to take leave of the subject, this occasion should not be missed. If the idea—to overstate, exaggerate, and accentuate, as suggested by Arendt's method—is to think the turn between *verticality* and *inclination*, then the maternal stereotype should be reinterrogated and exploited to its fullest potential. Stated differently: the prejudice must be transformed into an unprejudiced capacity for judgment.

The figure of the Madonna and Child, portrayed by innumerable artists and disseminated in thousands of churches, museums, and streets, is not just a Christian icon that melts the hearts of the faithful; it is, above all, a popular and hyperrepresented image of maternity that no relational ontology can put aside with impunity. Stereotypes, after all, don't always function as stumbling blocks for the free and disenchanted labor of the concept. Some stereotypes, such as that propagated in the iconology of the Virgin Mary, in fact have a great critical potentiality that risks remaining concealed precisely because they are too exposed. To exploit it properly, however, one must accentuate the emotional and sentimental baggage of this figure so as to fix and crystallize it into a form—a simple, oblique line, the relational sign of a specific posture. Or again—and this is precisely the challenge—one must geometrically distill the rhetoric of maternity and superimpose it, like a transparent screen, over the rhetoric of the philosophical subject, in order to highlight the differences between the two ontological, ethical, and political models. In the case of the maternal stereotype, which is in direct contrast with the verticalizing geometry of the autonomous subject and its possible symmetrical refraction, we are in the presence of a scene in which the vulnerable par excellence, the infant, not only unilaterally consigns itself to the other, but also, and more importantly, provides for originary bending, for a certain anomalous slope, for a posture. It is as if the fundamental concept of ethics were now seen, despite ages of sermons on moral uprightness, from the perspective of the vulnerable—or, more to the point, inclination. Or better: as if the ontology of the vulnerable, finally freed from the subject's belligerent masks, could count on the persistence of a popular imaginary that imposes an emotional pause and a mute resistance against the long record of violence.

Naturally, this is not what the young Benjamin meant in the fragment cited earlier. His reference to Kant, perhaps accompanied by Arendt's notes on the geometry of the subject, nonetheless allow us to push our inquiry in precisely that direction, or at the very at least allow us to regard the problem of inclination with curiosity. In fact, as one learns from his writings, Kant did not love mothers, children, or nannies, and, like most male philosophers, he was an unrepentant bachelor, easily bothered by crying children.

Which, all things considered, is actually a promising sign.

1

Barnett Newman

Adam's Line

I should demand the invariable application
to individuality, this day and any day, of
that old, ever-true plumb-rule of persons,
eras, nations.

Walt Whitman, *Democratic Vistas*

AT THE TATE MODERN IN LONDON, the abstract art lover can admire two paintings by Barnett Newman (1905–60): *Adam* (1951) and *Eve* (1950) (see Figure 1). The story of the founding couple of Genesis is one of the best-loved themes in all of art history and, over the centuries, has been represented in very different ways. Nevertheless, there is a certain constant element despite the diversity. In general, or at least in the traditional iconography dedicated to the story, Adam and Eve tend to appear together and mostly naked: at times they are innocent and immortal, at times ashamed and damned, driven from Paradise and on the way to mortality. Following a minor thread, Newman instead separates them, dedicating a distinct canvas to each of them. This choice breaks the couple and focuses attention more directly on sexual difference.

In *Adam*, a painting of considerable size, a red vertical stripe stands out against a blackish background, while two other red vertical lines—one thick, one thin, as though replicating through differing

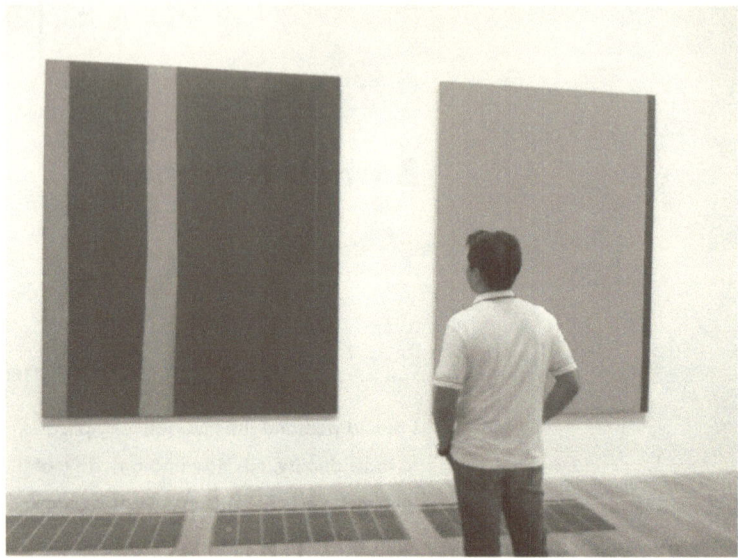

Figure 1. Barnett Newman, *Adam* (1951) and *Eve* (1950). Oil on canvas; 2429 × 2029 mm, 2388 × 1721 × 50 mm, respectively. Tate Modern, London.

thicknesses the concept of red verticality—appear at each side of the canvas. The entire surface of *Eve*, a painting of almost the same size, is invaded by a red monochrome, whereas a thin, dark, straight stripe appears on the canvas's right border. For Newman, evidently, the vertical axis is decisive for representing the first man, but only marginal when it comes to representing the first woman. This, at least, is what appears from an immediate comparison of the two representations. But of course, it is by no means certain that Newman is working with the intention of representation. Abstract art, as we know, involves complex problems that often trouble even specialists in the field. This nevertheless rarely discourages the untrained eye, which often feels entitled to take bigger liberties. Everything, obviously, depends on the claims. Here the claims don't aspire to art criticism; nor are they overambitious. I simply take Newman's paintings as symptoms—or, if you wish, as effective illustrations of a conception of the human that insists in an explicit mode, even emphatically, on verticality.

In Newman's canvas, Adam, the first man, indeed seems to evoke an essential and constitutive verticality—the same that, according to the painter, would lead the observers to recognize themselves in the upright posture, just as peculiarly human, which they assume as they stand before the picture. Eve, for her part, seems to invoke an overflow or a void, even more so because of the vertical stripe that appears at the canvas's margins, which perhaps interrupts, organizes, or controls the rest of the canvas. Art experts know that Newman's work is characterized by vertical bands set against monochrome backgrounds. His masterpiece, *The Stations of the Cross* (1958–66), consists of a series of paintings that obsessively repeat the theme of vertical stripes. According to some critics, there are even more specific reasons for his painting of Adam. As the Tate website explains, Newman's inspiration for his portrait of Adam derives from his familiarity with the Hebrew story of creation, but perhaps also from the etymology of the name *Adam*, which is linked to terms such as *earth*, *red*, and *blood*, and from the doctrine that sees God and man united in a single vertical light beam that rises between the earth and the sky. The name *Eve*, meanwhile, which is approached with some caution by linguists, is related to the etymological root for the term *life* and means "mother of the living."[1] More than any etymological suggestion, the relevance of these paintings consists of their colors and geometry. From this point of view, the schema seems explicit: what distinguishes Adam from Eve, in the confrontation suggested by Newman's work, is the accent on verticality in the representation of Adam. This very conspicuous verticality opens up two basic meanings, each consistent with the other. The first relates, in a naturalistic way, to the specificity of the human upright posture. The second, meanwhile, refers to the straight vertical line as the essential form of man's union or relation with God. In both cases, it is easy to argue, the spatial arrangement attributed to man is, structurally, a dimension that elevates him, making this elevation, this vertical rise from earth upward to heaven, the very mark of humanity. Adding a touch of mischief to the question of the comparison between Newman's *Adam* and *Eve*, one may ask why Eve is deprived of the vertical line, since she too walks upright, hence sharing with Adam the human tendency to rise toward God. Why then a void instead of a monumental straight strip? Why a homogenous color instead of a rising bar? A plausible response is not difficult to formulate: as sustained by a certain theological tradition, woman belongs to the human species, but does not represent the human in its full and originary sense.

The thesis, part of the patriarchal symbolic order, is so well known that it will suffice to summarize it in a few words. Differently articulated in different epochs, preceding the Bible and persisting in the event of abstract art, this tradition maintains that the human genre finds its essential paradigm in man [*uomo*], understood as male.[2] The human subject is then molded around him. From this point of view, Newman's paintings do not break with the patriarchal canon but indeed confirm it. They have the merit, however, of expressing that canon emphatically through the mythologeme of the vertical line. If it is true that abstract art is conceptual in nature, then the perpendicular axis that organizes Newman's canvas not only illustrates the fundamental ontology of verticality but also blatantly exposes its concept. In a certain sense, the problem of the two sexes is unresolved in his didactic schema, and remains superficial, quite simplistic, and disappointing. Setting aside the impact on the eye of the color red, Newman's painting of Eve disappoints: it appears as a void, as if the canvas were awaiting a figure the mark of which would also give form to woman. Respecting the artist's style, this could perhaps happen by drawing another line: not vertical but oblique and unbalanced, so as to mark the difference and not, as Newman has, to lose sight of it. In the coupling of humanity's fateful ancestors, man would be marked by verticality, and woman by inclination.

Stairs (1929) is a black-and-white photograph by the Russian constructivist Aleksandr Rodchenko (1891–1956) (see Figure 2). A series of oblique parallel stripes—an almost geometric grid—traverse the visual field. These are not lines painted by an abstract artist; they are precisely huge stairs photographed at an angle the perspective of which tilts them in comparison to the image's orthogonal frame. The intention of the constructivist artist is explicit: the regular alternation of the white stairs with their shadows transforms them into oblique bi-colored

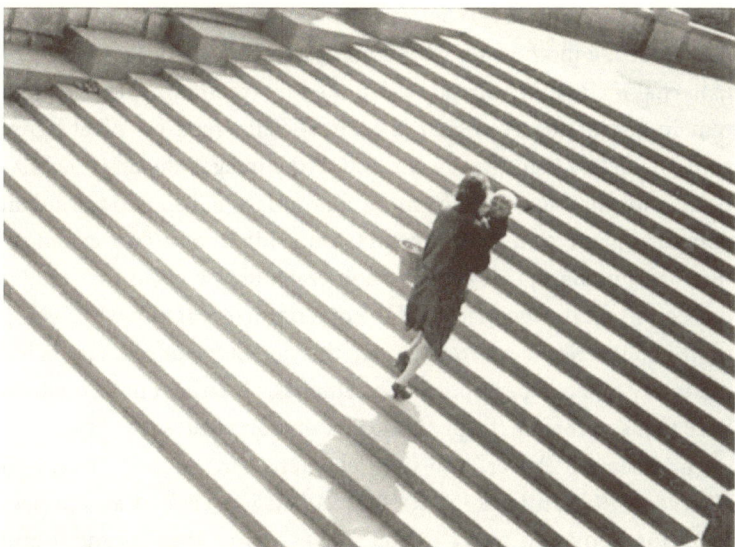

Figure 2. Aleksandr Rodchenko, *Stairs* (1929). Photograph. Copyright Rodčenko and Stepanova Archive, Moscow.

stripes that, at first sight, lose their three-dimensional character and instead appear flat. At the image's center, a woman goes up the stairs, hinting at the three-dimensionality of the stripes. The angle of the perspective makes her too appear inclined, oblique. The emphasis on inclination is notable, rendering this shot paradigmatic: in this photograph, there are no horizontal or vertical lines. By focusing on the opposition between the diagonal lines of the stairs and the woman, the image challenges the familiar law of gravity. In fact, because of a well-known optical illusion, the opposing inclinations are each accentuated. The oblique line thus organizes the entire space of the image, and in a very conspicuous way. The intent is clearly geometric, but it is a geometry that is antiverticalist, instead exalting inclination. It can thus even be assumed that the choice of a woman rather than a man may not be random; above all because the figure going up the stairs is a mother.

Carrying groceries with one hand, the classic index of the nourishing role destined to her by her sex, the woman in the photograph also carries a child. This is not just any man or any woman, a passerby, but, indeed, a mother, a nurturer and caretaker—an ordinary case of maternal inclination, already celebrated by tradition, who seems to remain fascinating even for the art of socialist realism. What figure could be better than this, in the end, if the image's theme is inclination? And what sign could be more appropriate, if disposed toward an oblique organization of the geometrical field? Upon closer examination, the human figures in this photograph are two, and the smaller one counts on the inclination of the other, who holds him while going up the stairs. Not at all emphasized, the stereotype of self-sacrificing maternity is barely perceptible. The emphasis is rather on the inclined lines that summarize the platitude in a simple posture.

In "Paternal Power," the sixth chapter of the *Second Treatise of Government*, John Locke notes that "Adam was created as a perfect man, his body and mind in full possession of their strength and reason."[3] Eve, one may assume, was also created in the same way, but the English philosopher does not mention it. In this chapter, Locke's intent is to emphasize how, after Adam, the prototype of an immediately complete humanity, "the world is peopled with his descendants, who are all born infants, weak and helpless, without knowledge or understanding."[4] The observation is, in many ways, obvious, but it takes on a specific meaning in the context of Locke's thought. More than representing a precarious stage of human existence—an especially precarious stage, given that Locke was writing in an age of high infant mortality rates—the philosopher considers infancy an "incomplete state": only when the infant becomes a free and rational individual has man reached his complete and perfect form. Having been created directly by God, Adam incarnates the exemplary human, all the more perfect because he was never an infant. His descendants, born of woman since the Fall, instead undergo a long period of minority, during which their lack of intellect exposes them above all to a total dependence. Based on this principle, Locke explains the natural basis of paternal power, or better of the temporary power of both parents, which consists in the obligation to "preserve, nourish, and bring up the children" until, having become adults, they acquire the status of "free and intelligent" agents.[5] Even if he continues to call it "paternal power," he concedes that "the mother too has her share with the father."[6] He even goes as far as to wonder if it wouldn't be more appropriate to call it "parental power."[7] However promising it may seem, the wording "parental power" remains a mere formula, a sort of verbal hypothesis that does not change the conceptual structure of Locke's theory, which then proceeds to make the usual argument in favor of man's natural superiority, or rather, of the superiority of hus-band over wife. On the topic of the two sexes, despite some moments of openness to a different view, even the undisputed father of modern liberalism thus aligns himself with the traditional canon. In Locke's imaginary, Adam—not Eve—is the archetype of the human that God has preserved from infantile imperfection to produce a model of full-blown rationality. The framework is still patriarchal, as some parts of the text demonstrate. Being "the abler and the stronger of the two," it is natural that the husband prevails over the wife when it comes to a "common decision."[8] It is natural, as well, that the father's authority provides the children with "a discipline necessary to their education."[9] It is indeed the father who takes responsibility for the crucial pro-cess that brings the creature, still lacking intellect, to become a fully free and rational individual—or, if you will, as an I in the full sense: a subject. For Locke's political anthropology, after all, this is the only thing that really matters. United by an enterprise that God seemed to reserve only to their sex, the protagonists in this scene are the father and the son, replicas of the same sex, just like the divine Father and Son. As for the nourishment and survival of the "helpless and weak children" of both sexes—this the English philosopher leaves to the mothers. Or this at least is what one may suppose, since Locke spends only very few words on this traditionally female task. Even though, in the terms of Locke's argument, maternity is indispensable, since we are discussing children and childhood, maternal inclination never-theless remains at the margins. Ignored at first, when the progenitors were still in Eden, and even after she became the mother of all liv-ing creatures on earth, Eve is never mentioned, not even through her sex. For Locke, it is therefore unlikely that maternal inclination could have anything to do with the process of perfecting the human whose endpoint is the free and rational individual. Even in modernity, which here announces itself in the first grammar of individual liberalism, the roles of the two sexes remain separate. As a sort of stereotypical figure frozen in a timeless tradition, the mother continues to occupy herself with vulnerable and dependent creatures, consigned by her natural inclination to care for the human pups. The father is the only protagonist of the new anthropologic turn. He educates the minors with all necessary discipline, and he invests himself in the difficult task of replicating himself in his son. In this way, he produces the autonomous I, self-sufficient and exemplarily vertical, in which the modern epoch decides to mirror itself. At a moment when modernity was still proud of itself, and not yet threatened by decline, persons, eras, and nations aligned themselves on the vertical line of this plumb-rule.

2

Kant and the Newborn

"To yourself, to yourself alone! That's the
whole of 'my idea,' Kraft!" I said ecstatically.
He looked at me somehow curiously.
"And you have this place: 'to yourself'?"
"I do."

Fyodor Dostoevsky, *The Adolescent*

What great philosopher hitherto has been
married? Heraclitus, Plato, Descartes,
Spinoza, Leibniz, Kant, Schopenhauer—
they were not; more, one cannot even
imagine them married.

Friedrich Nietzsche,
On the Genealogy of Morals

IN THE MODERN ERA, the most rigorous theorist of the free, rational, and autonomous self is Immanuel Kant, whose prototype of the
human is not far from Locke's. In one of his minor works, "Conjectures on the Beginning of Human History" (1786), we read that "if we
are not to indulge in wild conjectures we must begin with something
which human reason cannot deduce from prior natural causes—that
is, with the existence of human beings. These human beings must also

be fully developed for they have no mother to support them."[1] The influence of Locke's Adam is evident here. Being a "more or less selfish old bachelor,"[2] Kant does not like children. He laments the fact that, because children still lack reason and intellect, they "disturb the thinking section of the community"[3]—which is to say, him. Their mothers and nannies are also at fault: the child's "mangling of words . . . inclines them to hug and kiss him constantly,"[4] instead of rapping his knuckles. A good educator, of course, would not reward the lack of rationality expressed by the young child's babbling. Thinking that this deficiency makes a child even cuter, mothers and nannies instead reward the child with a warm embrace so that, in the end, this dynamic "must also be credited to the natural inclination of the nurses to comfort a creature that ingratiatingly entrusts himself entirely to the will of another."[5] Above all, therefore, what worries the philosopher of Königsberg, this most noble father of liberalism, is the relationship between the mother's inclination and the infant's dependence. This reveals that, underneath Kant's understandable annoyance at the noise of children, there lurks a philosophical problem. Infancy, understood as a state of immaturity [*minorità*] and dependency, is measured and, so to speak, crushed by the Kantian paradigm of a self who is autonomous, free, and rational—who controls his own inclinations and does not need others to incline lovingly toward him. This framework allows us to understand Kant's anguish over the maternal complacency that risks slowing down the self's development toward the adult state of rationality and autonomy. This same framework allows for the denunciation of the natural inclination, typically female, for a human creature who is in need of care and remains in a state of dependency. In essence, Kant condemns children not only because they are not yet adults, but also because they do not seem to be in any hurry to grow up. He blames women, meanwhile, because they are naturally inclined to appreciate and nurture this creature who depends on the care of others, and more precisely, on the care of woman. Between mother and child, here understood as a larval self who is not yet autonomous, a worrisome complicity therefore emerges. For those who are able to notice it, this is symptomatic of a question of geometrical order—or, more exactly, of the oblique line prevailing over the vertical. The claim here, in effect, is that maternal inclination for the infant ends up retarding the process that will free the self from dependence and culminate in the figure of the autonomous self—the self, that is to say, who will function as his own moral legislator, and who, once he assumes a typically erect posture, will be balanced on the internal axis of his own "authentic self." The scene of the mother with the child evokes a relational model that is mostly asymmetrical and unbalanced. The Kantian self is instead like Adam: self-enclosed, it stands up on its own with no need for external support.

In Kant's ethical and anthropological writings, inclination (*Neigung*) is placed under the rubric of desires, and more generally under the affections that concern man as a natural being. According to the classical model initiated by Plato and denounced by Nietzsche, the philosopher of Königsberg understands man to belong to "two worlds,"[6] one hinged on reason, which secures an intelligible (supersensible) existence and makes him a free and autonomous self, the other hinged on a sensible existence that subjects him to natural laws. These laws essentially turn natural man into a pathological being—a being who is passive vis-à-vis the mechanics of instincts and inclinations. Kant defines inclination—an affection which man, precisely, suffers—as "a habitual sensible desire,"[7] or in other words, as a desire that, by occurring repeatedly, becomes a habit. From this point of view, Kant observes, inclination comes dangerously close to addiction, which is to say, to "a physical inner necessitation to proceed in the same manner that one has proceeded until now."[8] A predicament of this kind is nauseating because "here the animal in human beings jumps out far too much, and that here one is led *instinctively* by the rule of habituation, exactly like another (non-human) nature, and so runs the risk of falling into one and the same class with the beast."[9] Understood in Kantian terms, this is an especially alarming problem. If, as a natural being, the self is a moral and rational creature who belongs to the species *Homo*—and so, is properly human—then this self would find it absolutely repulsive to be confused with beasts. This clarifies the philosopher's annoyance with mothers and children. They bother him because they are both borderline figures between the animal and human world: mothers because they pamper and care for human pups, and as such demonstrate an inclination that resembles the females of other species; children because, in essence, they still resemble animals. An extraordinary passage by Kant himself, however, resoundingly disproves this claim.

The passage, which is worth rereading, appears in a paragraph of *Anthropology from a Pragmatic Point of View* (1798), entitled "On the Inclination to Freedom as a Passion." This title is surprising, since it marks a meeting of the two worlds between which man is divided: the rational sphere of freedom and the natural sphere of passion. According to Kant, passion is "inclination that can be conquered only with difficulty or not at all by the subject's reason."[10] The formula is by no means new. It is, after all, an old story, already told by Plato and then handed down through the western philosophical tradition, about reason's famous inability to govern passions. What is new is Kant's definition of reason, which now has the quality of a "principle of autonomy" that, as a categorical imperative, imposes itself upon the rational self as the supreme principle of morality. Serving as a hallmark of modernity, the famous paradigm of the free and autonomous self—or, if you like, the subject whose rationality is indistinguishable from its capacity for self-determination—here enters the scene.

Individual freedom as autonomy and self-determination is also part of this framework. The attacks of passion against "pure practical reason," which is precisely this freedom, reach a point where freedom itself provokes, in the natural man, a specific passion. In the section in question, the philosopher illustrates his case in the following way: "Even the child who has just wrenched itself from the mother's womb seems to enter the world with loud cries, unlike all other animals, simply because it regards the inability to make use of its limbs as constraint, and thus it immediately announces its claim to freedom (a representation that no other animal has)."[11] Obviously, as Kant is forced to clarify in a note, not even the newborn has a representation of freedom. And how could he, since just after being born, he has no representations at all? He does have, however, "an obscure idea" of freedom,[12] as Kant puts it in a curious expression, which determines his desire to be free to such a point where it indeed manifests itself as a true and proper passion: he shows it when he is born, through loud cries, and a few years later, through his exasperated tears. Undoubtedly disturbing the thinking part of humanity, the newborn cries (so claims the philosopher) because he suffers the constraint of not being able to use his limbs, which is to say, because of his lack of autonomy. However obscure it may be, the idea of freedom is thus, according to Kant, innate in the human animal, whose first and annoying noise manifests its presence petulantly. His initial cry is neither a complaint for the separation from the maternal uterus, nor a heartfelt invocation by a defenseless and dependent creature.[13] It is, actually, a cry of indignation for not having being born already adult and perfectly autonomous—which is to say, free. As Tzvetan Todorov says, "if the newborn child cries, it is not to demand what is necessary for life and existence; it is to protest against his dependence in regard to others. As a Kantian subject, man is born longing for liberty."[14]

On this topic, a good family man like Hegel is more cautious. Observing the same phenomenon, Hegel writes that, "the child makes known its wants by screaming . . . in unruly, stormy, and peremptory fashion."[15] Revealing its conviction that "it has a right to demand from the outer world the satisfaction of its needs," the child's screams also reveal it to be "much more dependent and in much more need than the animal."[16] For Kant, by contrast, the angry cry of a child is essentially rage against his impotence and lack of self-determination. The accent falls, inexorably, on autonomy: the axiom that an individual who is autonomous is, as such, properly human—this individual that the child is not yet but will become—is nevertheless already present in the newborn's cry as his essence and destination. The same may be said of kids' crying, which is wrongly attributed to physical pain, and instead expresses the suffering caused by a condition that hinders free will: "This impulse to have his own way and to take any obstacle as an affront is marked particularly by his tone, and manifests a maliciousness that the mother finds necessary to punish, but he usually replies with still louder shrieking."[17] One should not be fooled by the ironic tone of Kant's pedantic but kindly genius: despite his amused levity, his discourse is philosophically serious. Indeed this levity, if traced on a biographical plane, can reveal otherwise serious motivations: perhaps the old Kant forgot that he was a child, or perhaps he never had the chance to care for an infant or another vulnerable and dependent creature. Or as we would say: he never inclined toward the other. Given that "the origin of the individual, birth and early child hood, for centuries belonged exclusively to a woman's universe,"[18] Kant lacked direct experience in this situation and in its attendant pathologies. Even though Kant shares this missed opportunity with many other philosophers, mostly bachelors, in his case the lack assumes a special prominence. His predilection for the category of autonomy, as an absolute criterion for defining the humanity of man, makes the matter completely particular to him. Hence, for Kant, the mere hypothesis of the human's structural dependence, even the human animal as a child, is gravely distressing. As the "metaphysical engineer of modern freedom,"[19] he cannot concede the existence of a human condition that would lack any trace of the principle of autonomy. His reference to the newborn's "obscure idea" of freedom responds to this need. As Foucault would say, it answers the very question that grounds the foundation of Kantian anthropology: "How to articulate an analysis of what the *homo naturalis* is on the basis of man defined as a free subject?"[20] The consequence is that when Kant focuses on children—and more generally on the phenomenon of tears, which is solely human but not solely infantile—he faces an embarrassing situation that leaves room for paradox.[21] In this sense, the inclination to freedom as passion, far from distressing only the infant, is an entirely Kantian pathology that manifests itself precisely as an absolute passion for the idea of autonomy—a passion to which Kant himself falls victim. He was described by his contemporaries as a sociable and likeable person; despite the limits of Königsberg, he was a citizen of the world. As a moral philosopher, he seems obsessed by an autistic model of a self that legislates from itself and upon itself—a straight and self-balanced self that takes its place in a straight line alongside every other self, over the earth's entire surface, all of which are likewise autarchic and at the same time replicas of one other. Perfectly homogenous, their sum testifies to the universality of the moral law.

Arendt expresses surprise in her notes: "it is most striking that in *The Critique of Practical Reason*, and in his other moral writings, Kant hardly can speak of *other people [Mitmenschen]*. It is really just about the Self and Reason functioning in isolation."[22] For Kant, in short, "the moral delimits the space in which I think. It is principally solipsistic."[23] For Arendt, solipsism is a very serious matter, and as a concept it sheds further light on the importance of her remark that "every in-clination turns outward, it leans out of the self in the direction of whatever may affect me from the outside world"[24] In this remark, it is in fact precisely the autarchic and solipsistic verticality of the Kan-tian self that is under attack. It is worth repeating that an inclined self is precisely a self that, by assuming an oblique posture, protrudes outside the vertical axis that allows it to stand balanced on its base and to rise in full autonomy. By pushing the self precariously toward this "outside," inclinations throw the self out of balance and move it away from its reassuring center of gravity, which, in the upright pos-ture, otherwise remains stably "inside" at "the center" of the figure. Ousted from the internal axis of its balance, from the plumb-rule of its stability, the figure also loses the characteristics that ensure its self-sufficiency (which, stated in a Kantian vocabulary, consist of freedom, autonomy, and independence). It is not by chance that Arendt points out, in the same text, that self-centeredness creates a very serious philosophical issue, especially for ethics. "How difficult this problem may be is gauged by the fact that religious commands were likewise unable to formulate their general moral prescriptions without turning to the self as the ultimate standard—Love thy neighbor as thyself, or do not do unto others what you do not want done to yourself."[25] This is aggravated in the case of Kant's categorical imperative, which makes the self its own legislator and releases it from divine commandments and heteronomic laws. By proclaiming the self's moral independence, Kant creates a self whose righteousness consists in obeying its own self-made laws and will: "an entirely autonomous person."[26] This type of self splits in two in order to give orders to its own self, with an imperative and categorical voice, a monologue in which the self addresses itself in the second person. The famous Kantian formula is "you must"; everything happens within the self. If this self had come into being through some sort of chromosome—if it were not pure form—we could attribute its existence to a "selfish gene" as distinct from an inclined subjectivity, which would hold an "altruistic gene." But this would ultimately only complicate the problem, since in the name of the purity of the categorical imperative, Kant condemns egoism as a pathology caused by "weak mole's eyes of selfishness."[27]

For the philosopher of Königsberg, self-love—just like love in general, whether erotic or sentimental—is an inclination, if not, decisively, a passion that, as such, belongs to human pathologies. Here too we encounter an old story, well known to philosophers and theologians, which draws on a long tradition to narrate *amour sui* as a condemnable vice. When Kant is the one telling the story, he ends by posing a completely special problem. As Arendt puts it: "the old yet strange notion that I can love myself presupposes that I can incline myself towards myself as I incline out of myself towards others, be they objects or people."[28] But Kant himself, as Arendt notes, maintains that "inclination means to be affected by things outside myself, things which I may desire or for which I may feel a natural affinity."[29] A paradox thus arises: self-love assumes the form of a very anomalous auto-affection, which is to say an internal inclination that contradicts the postulate, shared by Kant, that inclination is of external "provenance." This, in turn, confirms that the geometric coordinates that orient this particular framework—the relations of inside and outside, interior and exterior—are the essential node of the problem. If inclination consists of an oblique line that pushes the subject outside of its vertical axis, it is inapplicable in the internal relationship of the self with itself. In other words, if there is no other or others on the scene besides the self, if there is only just the self by itself, then there is no inclination in the proper sense. This, at least, would be the logic. Kant, however, absorbed by the project of building an absolute and independent egoity [*egoità*], proposes an even more rigorous logic. Within the ambit of pure practical reason, where self-referentiality is the basis of all principles, the philosopher does not in fact grant the self any inclination. Encapsulated in its for-mal uprightness, straight within itself, the austere moral subject does not incline, not even in on itself. If it does incline, perhaps seduced by the representation of its own happiness, then it ceases to be a moral subject: because it is externally affected by a representation, it is no lon-ger free and autonomous. The problem cannot be solved by appealing to the redoubling of the sensible and the supersensible: in the postural geometry of Kantian ethics, the principle of the autarchic verticality of the self has a strict character. Kant knows perfectly well that "inclina-tion means to be *affected* by things outside myself, things which I may desire or for which I may feel a natural affinity."[30] Hence his thought rigorously follows a model where the self, well-grounded on its axis, straight on the line of the plumb-rule, avoids inclining toward "objects or persons." Above all, as is clear, it avoids inclining toward persons. If this were to happen, a disquieting scene would commence in which an other depends on me, with the risk that I could, in turn, depend on another and, as if by a capricious infantile gesture, the whole theory of the subject's autonomy would topple over. It is possible that Kant's self might not have a selfish gene, but it definitely doesn't have an altruistic one. Children be warned: if there are no mothers or nannies around, there's no use in screaming. Unless, of course, you wish to function as a zoological sample of the axiom of free will, which in the end at least would have the advantage of marking you as a "coming" member of humanity.

3

Virginia Woolf and the Shadow of the "I"

What is an individual, a solitary individual,
if not a tree that grows without regard
for everything it suppresses and breaks,
grabbing all the nourishment, air, and sun,
a being that is fully justified in its nature
and its being?

Emmanuel Lévinas, *Difficult Freedom*

IN THE HISTORY OF THE SUBJECT, the verticality of the Kantian self, while not an exceptional case, is nevertheless an exemplary one. By giving free rein to the individualistic anthropology of modernity, it provides a representation of the subject that is austere and perfect. Before continuing our inquiry into this subject, and in order to reflect upon the different versions of the verticality of the postural geometry that philosophy at once presupposes and reworks at different moments in its history, we should take brief literary pause. Let's return to 1929, the year in which Rodchenko took his photograph. This time, however, let's return not to Russia but to the United Kingdom, near Fitzroy Square in London, in order to pay a visit to the Bloomsbury Group.

The previous year, Virginia Woolf had been invited to lecture in Cambridge on the topic "Women and the Novel." The two lectures she gave would be published the following year as *A Room of One's Own*.[1] The various themes that Woolf famously treated there have served as a precious source for the development of feminist theory, and for twentieth-century thought more generally. Among them, one is extremely interesting, especially when considered from a philosophical point of view.

The theme appears in the book's final chapter, where the author, after having spoken at length about the relationship between women and writing, starts commenting on the literature of her time, and describes her impressions of a new novel by a certain "Mr. A," a young contemporary author who remains unidentified but whom critics and readers appreciate greatly. Using an anachronism, we could say that he was the author of a best-seller. Besides being polemical, Woolf's tone is also deliberately ironic. Even so, she leaves room for an initial expression of enthusiasm and a declaration of relief. She confesses, in fact, that after immersing herself in novels written by women, "it was delightful to read a man's writing again." In Woolf's comparison of contemporary novels authored by both men and women, the former seem to have the upper hand, at least with reference to the contemporary novel. She adds that the mysterious Mr. A's masterpiece "was so direct, so straightforward after the writing of women. It indicated such freedom of mind, such liberty of person, such confidence in himself."[2] Woolf continues with other generously appreciative remarks, but the irony soon turns into open criticism:

> But after reading a chapter or two a shadow seemed to lie across the page. It was a straight dark bar, a shadow shaped something like the letter "I." One began dodging this way and that to catch a glimpse of the landscape behind it. Whether that was indeed a tree or a woman walking I was not quite sure. Back one was always hailed to the letter "I." One began to be tired of "I." Not but what this "I" was a most respectable "I"; honest and logical; as hard as a nut, and polished for centuries by good teaching and good feeding. I respect and admire that "I" from the bottom of my heart. But—here I turned a page or two, looking for something or other the worst of it is that in

the shadow of the letter "I" all is shapeless as mist. Is that a tree? No, it is a woman.[3]

The crucial phrase in this critical construction is obviously "it was a straight dark bar, a shadow shaped something like the letter 'I,'" which conveys perfectly the geometrical effect of the capitalized first-person pronoun. As Woolf notes, "I" isn't just a single letter; from a typographical standpoint, its most salient aspect is the single straight line—a stripe, as it were, or better a bar positioned vertically on the page's horizontal surface. Even for the distracted reader, its geometrical effect is clear or at least easily recognizable. To leave it at that, however, would be to remain on the geometrical field of the plane. In Woolf's eyes, by contrast, the picture becomes three-dimensional: the bar rises above the text and dominates it. By towering over the page like a dark bar, the "I" invades the text with its shadow and reduces it to an uncertain and blurred background. This is an optical phenomenon that the vertical "I" produces upon a planar surface. Or, one could say, it is an optical illusion that makes the dark bar appear as if it were lifting itself from the surface of the page, where it lies alongside the other letters, in order to obscure the other letters with its perpendicular shadow. This strange experience is more than just an effect of the eye's imaginative capacity (which is perhaps particularly fervid in those who live every day, as Woolf did, grappling with the signs of writing). Illusory or not, her vision has an immediate speculative meaning from a philosophical angle. Put simply, Woolf's passage offers philosophy an explicit critical perspective on the prevaricating geometry of the "I," which is finally nailed against the vertical axis of its arrogant posture. If it is true that the critique of the autopoietic configuration of the "I" characterizes a good part of the most refined philosophies of the twentieth century, then the passage in question amounts to a formidable resource. Far from presenting it as an oddity or an epiphenomenon, she turns the geometrical physiognomy of the "I" into a fundamental interpretive key for the deconstruction of the modern subject.

The close connection between writing and figure is obviously not a new discovery. In western alphabetic writing, which is far from the expressiveness of ideograms, words are nevertheless also figures, in-habiting the space of the page and in possession of their own geomet-rical physiognomy. It is in precisely this sense that the correspondence between the Italian *io* and English *I* creates problems. The Italian pro-noun *io* appears as a small word; in the good-natured rotundity of the second vowel, it is rounded and a bit potbellied. The English *I*, by contrast, stands alone: always capitalized, and without another vowel to accompany it, it is a self-sufficient and solitary letter. Woolf shows that it peremptorily assumes the austere air of a bar that is rigid and straight, not to mention solipsistic, autarchic, and solid. Although it lies horizontally upon the printed page, it seems to rise out of it into an upright position through a sort of congenital three-dimensional effect. As Woolf intuits, the vertical posture fits the "I" in a simple and perfect way, as if its typographic function were to synthesize in just one letter the quintessence of the *Homo erectus*—if not also, to put it bluntly, the phallic erection.

In effect, even without exploiting the double entendre, her thesis is quite explicit. Rigid, impermeable, and compact, the "I" positions itself perpendicularly against the page and always stays erect. Woolf, an attentive reader, notices the cumbersome consequence: the erect pronoun "I" ends up obscuring the other words. Verticality, crisp and clear-cut, is not only a sign of predominance but also, at the same time, the reduction of what "remains"—the other, what is not "I"—to something formless, and therefore inessential and unrecog-nizable. "Whether that was indeed a tree or a woman walking I was not quite sure,"[4] Woolf writes, hardly by accident, to highlight how the shadow of the "I" blurs all the other figures on the page. Not at all naïve, her conjecture is less bizarre than it may appear at first. The Woolfian imaginary—or better, her narrative technique—frequently employs slippage, transposition, and tricks. She is notoriously agile with metonymies and metaphors, and in order to understand her technique, one must have the patience to follow the game of her com-binatory art. In this case, the game is in plain view. First juxtaposed to woman, the tree—part of a celebrated iconographic tradition—soon comes to recall the figure of a man. Instead of being confused with the female figure, the result of this operation is that the image of the tree in Woolf's cited paragraph ends up highlighting the verticality of the "I," the arrogant dominance of the rigid and straight bar "and the aridity, which, like the giant beech tree, it casts within its shade."[5] The solitary and obscure bar, the self-satisfied dominance of the erected I, remains sterile: "Nothing will grow there."[6] Not only does this "I" blur the image of the other; by standing upright like a giant tree, it also produces between itself and the other the interval of a deadly zone.

On a superficial reading of these extraordinary pages, one perhaps could infer that masculine literary writing is characterized by the suffocating presence of the pronoun "I," whereas feminine literary writing is not. Because of the simple rules of the English language, of course, this is obviously not so; and, in any case, this is not what the author of *A Room of One's Own* meant. Her thesis is more daring and, in speculative terms, more interesting. Woolf suggests that, when comparing the written works of the two sexes, the solipsistic gigantism of the I—and of everything represented by the self-referentiality of the I and its sterilizing effects—is linked to the phenomenology of a subject that, during fascism, ends up exhibiting an "unmitigated masculinity" and "self-assertive virility."[7] The I that continuously straightens itself and rears itself up on principle, that claims to be autarchic, that fully enjoys its verticality, is in every sense an expression of "the strong sex." These characteristics—together with the obsessive repetition of the pronoun: *I, I, I* . . . —lead Woolf, while reading Mr. A's novel, to terrible boredom: "But why was I bored? Partly because of the dominance of the letter 'I,'" and partly, as Woolf certainly knew, because of the monotony of a historically authoritative framework in which the male paradigm has been dominating for centuries, and in various forms. The phenomenon is well known and, in the book in question, Woolf relates it directly to the age-old patriarchal tradition that attributes to man "feeling that one has some innate superiority."[8] This means, among other things, that when women, after being excluded for centuries, finally access knowledge, arts, and writing, they find themselves in the predicament of having to operate according to canons and styles that are foreign to them, because they have been decided by the other sex. Because the male writer's special relationship with literary tradition is so evident, Woolf has no hesitation in recognizing the male imprint on the novel she has been reading, and finds quite boring the symptoms of pronominal erection. In speculative terms, however, there is a silver lining to her boredom: precisely by observing and describing these symptoms, she ends up delivering philosophically sharp reflections on the subject's geometrical configuration and on verticality as its essential dimension. As Woolf notes, the "I" is straight, lone, self-sufficient, independent, domineering, deadly, and prevaricating. Focused on itself and wrapped around the rigid vertical axis of his erect posture, the "I" does not need others. Even without having read Kant, it is easy to see how these are questions that belong to philosophy: just replace the "I" with the most famous synonyms of philosophical language, and her observations fit perfectly with the individual or the subject. Or rather: to the oft-overlooked geometrical schema of their conception.

A great innovator and original writer, as well as a militant feminist, Woolf often has been placed among those writers who distrust women's emancipation and the egalitarian paradigm, and insist instead on sexual difference, or, if you will, on the question of gender difference. The theoretical framework of *A Room of One's Own*, which is focused on a comparison between men's and women's literature, provides a useful model of Woolf's reasoning on this matter. Her point is not merely to include women authors, leaving aside centuries of exclusion, to propose an asexual, universal, and neutral writing style. Instead, her objective is to mark the difference between the two sexes through a point-by-point analysis of their distinct universes of writing, and of the historical conditions that produced those distinctions. Raised "in the midst of that purely patriarchal society" that deemed them incapable of understanding or producing literature, Woolf points out that both Jane Austen and Emily Brontë "wrote as women write, not as men write."[9] As such, the two great British writers represent a general condition, applicable to all other women writers. In a patriarchal society, both men and women, whatever their talent, are at "the centre of some different order and system of life," but, as a consequence, the woman who writes has to "creat[e] in a different medium from his own."[10] From a certain viewpoint, it seems that this disadvantage may turn into an advantage: the historically determined sociocultural conditions that penalize women also end up stimulating women's creativity. "But this creative force differs greatly from the creative power of men,"[11] says Woolf with noticeable emphasis. At the same time, though, "perhaps a mind that is purely masculine cannot create, any more than a mind that is purely feminine."[12]

Woolf's argument is delicate in many senses, first of all because she here introduces the theme of the androgyne, which is of Platonic inspiration and which she also had developed in *Orlando* (1928). In *A Room of One's Own*, the theme appears even more delicate, as it introduces a brusque change of register. She goes from the primacy of history to that of essence, or, to say it more plainly, she moves from the thesis of gender as a cultural construction to the thesis that genders have a natural basis. Disengaged from the sociocultural context that seemed to determine their sense, the "feminine" and the "masculine" now become two atemporal essences, two complementary parts of an originary unity, which is to say the androgyne. This argument confirms the critique that Woolf's essay on "women and the novel" rests upon a somewhat rigid dualistic schema. The problem does, in fact, exist. If the two sexes are postulated as ideally complementary, rather than manifesting a difference determined by patriarchal society, which also influences their respective literary expressions, then the two sexes become, in the abstract, two sides of the same coin. In this case, one would expect that, after having pointed at the verticality of the I as typically masculine, the writer also would have remarked on a corresponding geometrical figure for the feminine. Surprisingly, this figure is instead lacking. The geometrical schema, in this case, does not function. It is incomplete.

Obviously, the point is not to accuse Woolf of essentialism and schematicism, or to ascribe to her a culpable omission, but to take advantage of this alleged schematicism in order to make them philosophically interesting. In brief: the challenge is to reclaim the theme of the virile verticality of the I in order to insert it in a geometrical system in which the other sex can find expression too. Woolf does not venture into this terrain. In *A Room of One's Own*, her discourse on the upright posture of the I as a specifically masculine mark is a brilliant intuition that did not achieve completion in a finished system comprehensive of both sexes. Once she acknowledges that the autarchic verticality of the straight bar is a characteristic of the male posture and of its impulsive erection, she says nothing about a specific female geometry that would complete the picture. One therefore remains curious: what then happens to women, and to the "feminine," in the patriarchal tradition that celebrates—literally as well as in literature—the *Homo erectus*? Is there a figure, a line, a characteristic trait that positions woman otherwise in the geometrical imaginary of western culture? What image—even stereotype—may correspond to the quintessence of the feminine within the scope of spatial representation?

Symptomatically, as Kant also knew, there is a plausible response to these questions. As already mentioned, many symptoms of the western macrotext lead us to believe that the geometrical sign of the female world relates to the inclined line, or, if you will, to inclination. As seen in one of the most tenacious stereotypes about women, women are characterized by maternal inclination, understood as a natural propensity to procreate and raise children, which supposedly would realize the true female essence. Kant was persuaded of this natural female inclination, even though he was somewhat bothered by the sound of it. It is worth noting that "inclination" can be defined as a "propensity," and that the two words, as we learn from dictionaries, function as synonyms. The inclined line is such because, departing from the barycentric vertical axis, it leans forward [*pende*]. In the case of the imaginary related to maternity, which the iconography of the Virgin Mary exalts and crystallizes, this materializes in the female figure who habitually leans [*pende*] over an infant, which is to say the other, who is completely vulnerable and hence dependent on the mother. Do not be bothered that the relational structure of this argument, drawing on etymology, aligns "pendency," "dependence," and "propensity."[13] The strategic advantage of reasoning through schemas, and of bringing to the extreme Arendt's already extremizing method, is the possibility of simplifying the relevant conceptual components. There is a resounding difference between the barren, erect bar on which Woolf meditates, and the inclined posture of the mother leaning over the child. By polarizing the two sexes, the design—the system, the schema—succeeds in completing itself: in this postural organigram, which is both simplified and confirmed by age-old stereotypes, man adheres to the vertical axis, whereas woman is predisposed to inclination. He is straight, solid, autonomous, and autarchic; he even keeps others at a distance by throwing a shadow on them. By contrast, she is inclined, unbalanced, and pendent; she leans naturally on others who require her proximity. In philosophical terms, to simplify the schema further and to paraphrase the language of genetics, one could speak of a selfish subject and of an altruistic subjectivity—the former model based on the joys of an autarchic I, and the latter that speaks instead to a primary relation and a state of dependency.

In *A Room of One's Own*, Woolf's contribution to the critical description of the first model is not only notable, but also philosophically valuable, and in its detached irony on the bar's pronominal erection, almost ingenious. While it proves problematic for the internal economy of her text, even the short mention of the androgyne, and hence too of Plato, proves interesting. Far from limiting her characterization to the modern subject, or to the specific figure of individualistic ontology, the paradigm of verticality had enormous success in ancient philosophy, including Plato, and has repeatedly returned if not strengthened over the course of the entire history of philosophy. Hence, rather than speaking of the vertical model of the subject, one should speak of the general model of a verticality that is also reflected in the modern subject's configuration. The point of retracing the verticalizing schemas that are the foundations of the various systems in the history of philosophy is to entirely deconstruct this same history, if not universal history itself. But this would be a titanic enterprise—as well as rather tedious. In order to avoid boredom and fatigue, it will suffice to test certain regions of the imaginary, to probe certain important and promising texts—and above all, in conformity with Woolf's homage to the ancient theme of the androgyne, to turn directly to Plato.

4

Plato *Erectus Sed* . . .

The fateful process of civilization would
thus have set in with man's adoption of an
erect posture.

Freud, *Civilization and Its Discontents*

HOMO ERECTUS, as defined by the discipline of anthropology to designate the privilege of the vertical posture, makes its entrance on the
philosophical scene before this name was even invented. The famous
Platonic myth of the cave speaks, among other things, to this too.

"There is something garish about the visibility of the naked creature who walks upright."[1] This claim appears in Blumenberg's monumental 1989 book on Plato's myth of the cave and the complex history
of its inexhaustible interpretations. For some, the fascination with this
myth derives from its attempt to narrate beginning: the cave could
be an allusion to the uterus (as in Irigaray's exemplary analysis),[2] and
the effort it takes to come out into the light, or it could allude to the
evocation of the initial phase of the process of hominization. Blumenberg, as distinct from Irigaray, is particularly interested in anthropologic and anthropogenic interpretations of the myth, but he elaborates
a different approach to the problem of beginning. From the point
of view of the history of man, he notes, the cave does not represent
the beginning but a phase that appears "at a relatively late point in

evolution."[3] The cave is already a refuge for *Homo erectus* "who, about twelve million years ago, had to leave the dwindling rain forest and venture into the savannah."[4] According to Blumenberg, certain bizarre elements of the Platonic cave—such as the fabrication of illusory images, simulacra, and shadows—are related precisely to this particular evolutionary stage. In his opinion, this was a phase when the males of the human species not only found a necessary refuge in caves, but also used them as a temporary resting place between the hunts they performed in the dangerous territory of the outside world. The world of the cave thus became, for them, a protected space for a sort of "boredom between hunting, plundering, and war."[5] In this phase of civilization, indeed, there is a type of selection that ends up weakening instead of fortifying the race. "Characteristics that had been possible and acceptable only within the cave slipped through the net of natural selection;"[6] hominids settle down stably in the cave's protected space and take up artistic and intellectual pursuits. These are, of course, exactly the strange activities in which the professionals of imitations and fabricators of simulacra specialize. The cave thus represents a new anthropologic type, as well as a new expression of the human adventure on the path to civilization. The first and fundamental weakening of the *Homo erectus* occurs between its walls.

Blumenberg's thesis reveals a somewhat Nietzschean influence, and it is worth paying attention to the great liberty with which he treats the evolutionary paradigm, making the category of *Homo erectus* available for philosophical uses (although not without a certain forcing). In the Platonic myth, there is indeed a man who conquers the erect posture, but this has nothing to do with the history of hominization or with the evolution of the human species in any technical sense. If it is true that life in the cave is rather boring, this tedium—but also falsity and annoying futility—does not emerge from a contrast with the wild and violent life of predatory man. It results instead from a contrast between life inside the cave and the theoretical experience of the authentic philosopher (the myth's protagonist), who leaves the cave to face the theoretical world of the outside. A solitary contemplator of ideas, he justifiably denounces his rivals in the education of the Greeks, which is to say the poets, artists, and sophists who unfortunately excel in the creation of useless puns and false appearances. This rivalry for cultural hegemony in Athens, however, counts as only one side of the story. The more fundamental point pertains to the very nature of the human (*anthropine physis*), which, here as in other crucial moments of Plato's production,[7] raises a decisive question. Symptomatically, the figure of the *Homo erectus* plays a role in this question, despite its absence from Blumenberg's analysis. By illustrating the characteristics of a new *anthropos* belonging to the philosophical race, the myth tells the story of how he leaves behind the Athenian cave dwellers to stand up and remain upright.

Imagine an underground cave—Socrates says in the *Republic*—where there are men who "are in it from childhood with their legs and necks in bonds so that they are fixed, seeing only in front of them, unable because of the bond to turn their heads all the way around."[8] They are in an awkward position: bent over themselves, their posture is forced, vile, uncomfortable, and ignoble. All they can see is a sequence of shadows on the wall in front of them. Unable to turn their heads, they are prisoners of a complex mechanism of illusory images. One of the cavemen, though—Socrates continues—frees himself from the shackles and stands up, abandoning the humiliating posture that hitherto had forced him to the ground. This man finally stands up: the first conquest of the liberated prisoner is the erect stance. Thus does *Homo erectus* make its appearance in the Platonic myth. This same man, now able to turn his head around, then discovers the trick of the shadows produced by strange puppeteers, specialists in illusion, and starts walking toward the cave's entrance. The road is uphill and the man advances with difficulty; this is, after all, the first time he has walked. His eyes, above all, suffer from the change of light; he is dazzled by the rays that penetrate the cave from the entrance. The spectacle of what is outside—trees, lawns, ponds, the high and glowing sun—is magnificent. His eyes gradually adapt. Then comes the climax of Plato's story: the liberated man stands firmly under the perfect midday sun, its rays perpendicular and hence producing no shadows. He turns his eyes to the sun and is able to contemplate it without being blinded, recognizing it as the principle of everything that is visible. The protagonist of this adventure has now become a philosopher—or better, he has become *the* Platonic philosopher, who is champion of a new anthropological type. Plato is, after all, competing with other "wise men" to give Greek culture a new paradigm of human nature, other than the ones provided by epic and tragedy, and his philosophy is the model of this paradigm. In the architecture of the *Republic*, the myth of the cave has been introduced precisely to explain what the true philosophy is, presupposing the famous analogy between the visible and intelligible orders. The sun corresponds to the idea of Good: "as the good is in the intelligible region with respect to intelligence and what is intellected, so the sun is in the visible region with respect to sight and what is seen."[9] In the development of the narrative, the conquest of the erect posture in the cave was an announcement and a sort of premonition. Only after having reached his destination—only when he is contemplating the Good while standing erect on the axis of truth—does the new man, the philosopher, become truly erect. Satisfied by his vertical posture, he wishes to remain there forever, and he is not willing "to go down again among those prisoners or share their labors and honors, whether they be slighter or more serious."[10] Socrates's story, though, does not end here. The philosopher does turn around, returning down to the strange circus in the cave. Once arrived, with suffering eyes and no longer accustomed to the strange habits of the cavemen, he warns the prisoners about the falsity of their visions and, unfortunately, frees them from their shackles. His return then comes to an unhappy end: they kill him. The myth concludes on an enigmatic note: it would have been better for the philosopher had he stayed in the world above instead of going back down to the cave below.

To retrace the history of the vertical subject, the myth of the cave is a very significant point of departure. It narrates the philosopher's difficult climb to exit the cave and contemplate, in the open, the sky of ideas. By directing his eyes to the sun, which is to say the Good, he stands vertically on the perpendicular axis of truth. This is the entrance on the scene, in ancient Greece, of the *philosophus erectus*. The narrative of the myth of the cave is organized along the spatial coordinates of low (*kato*) and high (*ano*). Beyond its various metaphorical valences, in the elementary structure of this myth, low and high function as geometrical points to designate two types of lines—one inclined, the other vertical. The path that leads from the subterranean cave to the earth's surface, on which the philosopher first climbs up and then down, is oblique. Low and high here simply define the slope [*pendenza*] of the path on which the philosopher goes up and down. The line the philosopher follows when, finally outside, he stands straight and steady, staring at the glaring midday sun, is vertical. In this case, high and low define the perpendicular line between sky and earth, which has its apex in the luminous star, and hence too in the idea of the Good, which is the very principle and zenith of the intelligible. By joining in with the story's plot, the myth narrates two types of ascent: one is characterized by movement and two-way travel, the other is static, a perfect verticalization. Both ascents are of a philosophical sort; both also evoke the Orphic-Pythagorean tradition. But while the first (*anabasis*) alludes to the graduate rite of passage that leads man to philosophy, the second (*epopteia*) relates to the pure and sublime form of philosophy that Plato identifies with noetic contemplation.[11] Within the economy of the myth, it is obviously the second that verticalizes the philosopher—or, if you will, the philosophizing subject, this new model of *anthropos*. Not as obvious, and actually problematic if not enigmatic, is the reason why the *philosophus erectus*, after having gained the contemplative posture through a difficult ascent, would have to abandon it to go backward, with just as much difficulty. More than a technical difficulty, both the ascent and the descent entail pain and suffering for the philosopher's eyes because of the transition from darkness to light, and vice versa. It is also very painful for the philosopher to decide to leave the immobile verticality of a true day in order to return to the cave. He does not then re-descend voluntarily. Or—and this is precisely the enigma—he perhaps does not re-descend at all.

Defined by Socrates as an image, the myth of the cave is also a story, or better, a story with a strong biographical component. The philosopher who goes back down into the dark cave, and who the cavemen kill after he has freed them from their chains, clearly evokes

Socrates himself. The pure contemplator, verticalized on the axis of the Good and immobile in his sublime and solitary visions, evokes Plato. Their two biographies mingle and blur together. Multilayered and open to different interpretations, the myth thus also narrates the biographical plot that binds the two philosophers. This is not a mere superimposition of characters who end up complicating even more the story's already intricate symbolism. Plato's strategy is daring and subtle, and it even has an emotional feature. Through a clever narrative montage, he stages a problem that touches him in the first person, that profoundly anguishes him, and that, in the myth's polysemy, is perhaps even the decisive question. The main challenge is in fact the distinction between the philosophical life, understood as a practice and a style of existence, and philosophy understood as an educational process (and above all as *theōria*, noetic contemplation). By putting the two face to face, the myth questions their compatibility, and also the different meanings of philosophizing that Socrates and Plato represent and, in a sense, incarnate.

Foucault rightly notes that, in its Greek origin, "philosophy cannot be separated from a philosophical existence," such that "the practice of philosophy must always be more or less a sort of life exercise. . . . Philosophy is fundamentally not just a form of discourse, but also a mode of life."[12] The asymmetry between Socrates and Plato, staged through the enigmatic superimposition of their characters, should be analyzed on the basis of this very problem. The myth of the cave speaks to a rupture, to a confrontation between two different meanings of philosophy: the way in which, with his doctrine of ideas, Plato distances himself inexorably from Socrates, his teacher. The philosopher, frozen in the act of contemplating the idea of the Good, straight and solitary on the vertical axis that leads him to stare at the sun, alludes to a philosophy that is no longer a way of life but now instead a discourse—or better, abstract theory, nondialogical construction, episteme, science. With Plato, as Arendt might put it, the *bios theōrētikos* replaces the *bios politikos*.[13] The solitary thinking experience, now identified with pure *theōria*, substitutes for the interactive exercise of a philosophy that, with Socrates, was genuine political practice. The verticality of the Platonic theoretic model prevails over the horizontality of Socrates's political model. In this mise-en-scène, the tension between the two models is still tragic and unresolved. If, in the myth of the cave, the contemplator redescends into the cave, he does so with nostalgia not only for an erect, no-etically correct posture, which he would not want to leave, but also for his teacher, Socrates, who he mourns and cannot forget. Whether it is Plato or Socrates who goes back down to the cave remains an enigmatic dimension to the myth that is left deliberately equivocal and emotionally suspended. From the point of view of the history of the subject's verticality, the effect of the Platonic imaginary doesn't leave any room for doubt. When the vertical subject implants itself in *theōria*, it puts down deep roots. Inside the cave where Plato's teacher tried all his life to free the Athenians, and suffered the consequences, now the contemplator, having put aside the Socratic mode of politics, limits himself to sketching the "perfect *polis*," entrusting its realiza-tion to a fortunate circumstance whereby kings become philosophers and philosophers kings. This is, indeed, Plato's return. He decides not to partake in the risks of political action; instead, as Arendt observes, he founds on a theoretical basis the discipline that will come to be named political philosophy.

Even though the myth of the cave has a clear political dimension, it is common to think that it describes above all the philosopher's progress—or, if you will, the progress of the man of which the phi-losopher is the archetype—toward attaining consciousness of the truth. In the immense critical literature on this question, Heidegger's position stands out. In the early 1940s, he published "Plato's Doctrine of Truth."[14] The complex thesis of this text, which he also developed elsewhere, is that the essential comprehension of the truth (*alētheia*, or better, *a-lētheia*, which Heidegger translates as "un-hiddenness" [*Unverborgenheit*] and "un-concealment" [*Entborgenheit*]) suffers a transformation with Plato. According to the German philosopher, in the story of the cave, *alētheia* loses its original meaning of "uncon-cealment" and instead becomes *orthotes* (correctness), the gaze's right-ness relative to its object. Speculatively acute, Heidegger's comments remain useful even in isolation from the context of his argument, freed from the grip of Heidegger's formidable theoretical apparatus. Curiously, the term *orthotes* is not present in the Platonic text on which Heidegger here is commenting—even though it certainly is not unknown to Plato, who uses it in *Cratylus* with reference to the "correctness of names."[15] Here as elsewhere in his dialogues, Plato normally uses the adjective *orthos*, as well as its adverbial form, in the common sense of "straight" and "upright." A banal term in the language of everyday life, this word nevertheless gives rise to a conceptual itinerary that is nothing short of sensational. Heidegger, to be sure, provides an interesting definition. During a course on the myth of the cave he taught in Freiburg in 1931–32, later published as *The Essence of Truth* (1943), he writes in a note: "ὀρθός [*orthós*] (rectus—right): straight, without diverting, without detour; not by way of the shadows, the thing itself."[16] The accent is thus on a concept of straightness that avoids insisting on the aspect of verticality.[17]

It is no small task to reconstruct the term's history and to grasp its essential facets. On the one hand, *orthos* and its derivatives—*rectum* (Latin), *droit* (French), *dritto* and *retto* (Italian), the English words *right* and *straight*, and so on—have an ordinary meaning that is immediately understandable. On the other hand, however, these terms reside at the origin of a series of philosophical, theological, ethical, and juridical concepts that, starting from the Greek *orthos logos* and running through to the Latin *recta ratio* ("right reason"), not only inform the technical vocabulary of the law ("right" in English, *diritto* in Italian, *Recht* in German, *droit* in French, *derecho* in Spanish), but also indicate moral rectitude or righteousness. One should add, pleonastically, that already in Greek, as in the modern languages that have inherited its words, *orthos* is usually also understood as a synonym for "right" [*giusto*] understood as that which is "correct." Aside from his complex disquisitions on *alētheia*, in other words, Heidegger here put his finger on a decisive problem: there is a strong connection between "truth" and "right."

Annoyed by Heidegger, and perhaps even more by Heideggerianism, Foucault treats the term *alētheia* with caution. He notes, among

other things, that one of the adjectives that most often accompanies
truth (*alēthēs*) is *euthus*, which is to say a common term that again
means "straight," even if it does not share its etymological root with
orthos.[18] It is useful to add that *euthus* has also a meaning related to
time: "immediately," "imminently," "without hesitation." One embarks
on the straight path, which is also the shortest distance between two
points, immediately, without wasting time. Foucault, however, does
not engage with considerations of this sort or with etymologies. In
a sentence that nicely sums up his thesis, he writes that "by virtue of
the fact that it is without deviation, concealment, mixture, curvature,
or disturbance (it is really straight), this unconcealed, unalloyed, and
straight truth can thereby remain what it is in its unchangeable and in-
corruptible."[19] Even in the Foucauldian text, therefore, the aspect of
verticality remains untouched: in this text there is no mention of the
myth of the cave, even though Foucault frequently cites the *Republic*
and other Platonic texts. It is likely that this omission is due to Foucault's tense relation to Heidegger's philosophy, and in particular to its
clichés on the question of *a-lētheia*. Besides, these are posthumously
published lectures, written for the occasion and not intended for publication. It is significant, in any case, that Foucault chose to discuss
the concept of *euthus* instead of *orthos* with reference to *alētheia*.
Although both words relate to the notion of "right," and hence seem
to be synonyms, it is mainly *orthos* that characterizes the philosophical itinerary that brings the meaning of "straight and vertical" into
Christian theology and modern philosophy. Consulting the Greek
etymological dictionaries, one also learns that *orthos* and its lexical
family relate to a straight object lifting itself up, which extends to the
obscene sense of the phallus's "erection" or "straightening."[20] The same
can be said of *euthus*, with respect to the meaning of "ithyphallic." The
silence that both Heidegger and Foucault maintain with respect to the
spectacular mechanism of verticalization narrated by Plato's *Republic* could also therefore perhaps be read as a sort of reticence. This is
perhaps a bit mischievous, but it leaves intact the seriousness of the
problem. Given how peremptorily and clearly the representation of
truth as the perfect coincidence between verticality and straightness

emerges in the geometry of the myth of the cave, the two authors' silence on the subject indeed continues to surprise.

In fact, in the Platonic doctrine of truth, authentic philosophy—*theōria*—takes the shape of an immobile and ecstatic verticalization. This explains, among other things, why the prisoners are chained in a position that forces them "to see," and why their curled-up posture, bent over themselves, is related to the falsity of their "visions." The myth thus lends itself to a rereading through a narrative sequence that relates vision to posture. In the first event of the narration, a man stands up and changes the direction of his gaze: one of the prisoners is "suddenly forced to stand up [*anastasthai*], turn his head and look up [*anablepein*] at the light."[21] One has to wait until the end of the road that leads upward toward the sun—the brightest star and the zenith of the visible—for this initial event to turn into the philosopher's theoretically correct vertical posture. In this sense, the posture of this figure—in which the myth culminates and which deploys the Platonic geometry of truth—affects the concept of *orthos* more deeply than etymology can explain. If, in other words, there is such a thing as a Platonic *orthotes*, it does not reside in the body of the text but in the power of the image that presents it: the philosopher straightening up according to the perpendicular line of the truth.

On a philological plane, a passage from the *Timaeus* contains clues worthy of attention. At the end of the dialogue bearing his name, Timaeus gives a long speech on the cosmos's origin and structure. He speaks of man as a living being (*zoon*) and illustrates the parts and functions of the body (*soma*). Then he briefly mentions the question of the soul (*psyche*), confirming that its best part is the noetic: when the maker had to find a place for it, he placed it in the highest part of the body, the head. "The sovereign part of the human soul," Timeaus observes, "dwells at the top of the body, and inasmuch as we are a plant not of an earthly but of a heavenly growth, raises us from earth to our kindred who are in heaven."[22] Soon after those declarations, Timaeus reinforces them, immediately adding: "*Orthotata legontes.*" In other words: "these affirmation are very correct" (right, just). As so often happens in Plato's writings, he uses *orthos* in its general meaning of right, just, and correct. But the sentence that follows holds an interesting surprise. While continuing on to illustrate his thesis, Timaeus explains that "the divine power suspends the head and root of us from that place where the generation of the soul first began, and thus makes the whole body upright [*orthos*]."[23] In the space of a few lines, therefore, we find the same word, first used in its general sense, and immediately after that in the more specific meaning that evokes the vertical line. There are two reasons why this image is worthy of consideration. First, there is a connection with the so-called *arbor inversa* (reverse tree), a figure of a man who appears as an upside-down tree with its roots in the sky, an image that will enjoy great fortunes in medieval Christian treatises.[24] The second regards the use of the term *orthos* in the technical sense of erect posture. Although it is surprising and symbolically charged, the reversal pertains to the tree, not the man. The latter instead continues to hold his "normal" position as *Homo erectus*, even though his center of gravity is now no longer on his feet, but is perpendicular to his head, which attaches itself through noetic roots to the sky. A similar image may be found in Aristotle, who uses *orthos* to indicate the erect posture and also the same type of noetic attachment to the sky.[25] But it is above all in Plato, and more precisely in Plato's myth of the cave, that this image ends up assuming a meaning that is significant and particularly pregnant. After all, who else is the *philosophus erectus* if not the contemplator of ideas who connects his soul's eye to the sun (the Good) and hangs vertically from above? Who else but the philosopher—this figure who has straightened himself up according to the luminous axis of truth—has his head rooted in the sky of the intelligible and hangs from the heights of his pure thought? Who else except the new *anthropos*—finally connected to the verticality of theorizing and fixed in an atemporal state—no longer has his feet on the ground?

5

Men and Trees

Even in prayer he had stood erect, with an
air of conscious righteousness sufficient for
all his wants, and even some to spare with
which to judge others.

Elizabeth Gaskell, *Ruth*

IN CARL JUNG'S *Psychology and Alchemy* (1944),[1] there are two curious illustrations that appear under the label *arbor philosophica*, or
"philosophical tree." They reproduce two images from a fourteenth-
century manuscript, the *Codex Ashburnham*: a naked man lying on
the ground from whose penis grows a lush, straight tree, and a woman
in the same position from whose head grows a tree with a thinner
trunk (see Figure 3). Linking the two figures to the archetypes of the
unconscious he calls "anima" and "animus," Jung relates them to the
masculine and feminine versions of *prima materia* and identifies
them with Adam and Eve. Rich in details—among which are the sun,
the moon, the skull, the arrow, the hand, and more—the symbolic
framework that overloads the pictures is dense and lends itself to infinite interpretations. Jung's analysis is complex and completely internal
to his byzantine doctrine; but even a less refined eye than Jung's can
easily notice the contrast, somewhat cliché in iconographic history,
between the patriarch's penis that literally grows into a "woody" and

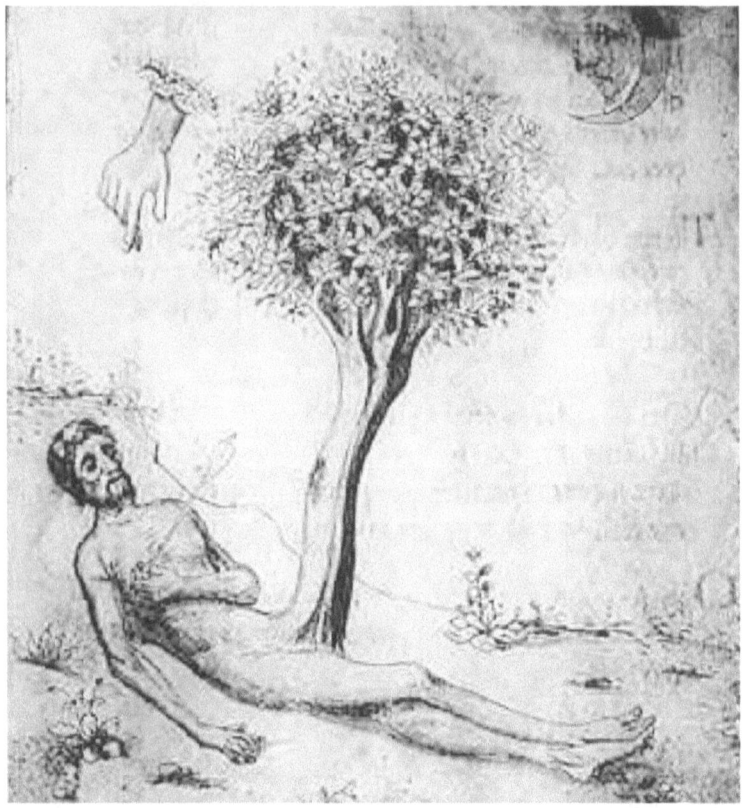

Figure 3. *Adam Pierced by the Arrow of Mercury* (from the *Miscellany of Alchemy, Codex Ashburnham,* 1166, f. 16). Laurentian Library, Florence, Italy.

the singularity of Eve who, in the alchemical version, watches a tree grow straight out of her head. As an authoritative tradition maintains, Eve symbolizes the earth, the nurturing and fecund *humus,* and hence life. Man, for his part, often appears in images that glorify his phallus. In medieval images, he is the ancestor whose genitals form the basis of the genealogical tree. The link between tree and phallus is very ancient but nonetheless documented, on a linguistic plane, through intriguing etymologies. For instance, the Jungian psychoanalyst James Hillman observes that "though all trees have been categorized as symbolically female because of their sheltering, nourishing, cyclical behavior, and because they provide the basic *hyle*, or matter, for so many human actions, the oak and the acorn were imagined as particularly male . . . because the acorn was called *juglans*, or glans penis of Jupiter."[2] Further, he continues, authors such as Aristotle, Pliny, and Celsus, "made this equation of penis-head and acorn, and fertility rites conjoined the mythological understanding of the oak with the morphological appearance of its fruit."[3] It is plausible that the same morphology also includes the rigidity of the erect penis. If it is true that woman is the womb of earth and flora, it is even truer that between man and tree there is a tight symbolic knot that often alludes to erection, not without a certain self-satisfaction.

In this sense, the verticality of the tree in the *Codex Ashburnham* betrays an exquisitely masculine imprint. As in Barnett Newman's abstract painting of Adam, which involves forms that are arboreal and blatantly ithyphallic, here too a straight bar rises. Even so, this does not exhaust the tree's enormous symbolic potential, which is capable of expressing itself on multiple registers. As Virginia Woolf well knew, the coincidence of verticality and erection is only the most banal face of the problem.

It is common knowledge that, already in ancient thought, the tree is the symbol of man himself, understood as a species. In many cultures, including the ancient Greek world and the Judeo-Christian tradition, the figure of the tree in fact signifies the vertical dimension, which is to say the natural disposition of a creature who rises on a straight line between the two poles of earth and sky. Equipped with roots, shaft, and branches, the image becomes even more complex. It comes to refer to the elaborate symbolism of the "cosmic tree" and—in Plato's *Timaeus*, as well as in the various doctrines that portray man as a "reverse tree"—often appears upside-down.[4] In these different contexts, which are crucially related to the paradigm of the ascension, verticality remains the essential characteristic of the figure, its densest symbol. According to the elementary nucleus of the symbol, man is imagined as a tree that stretches upward on a perpendicular line that also designates his "rectitude" and the "correctness" of his position vis-à-vis the order of the universe. The cosmic framework of which the symbol of the reverse tree is part ensures that the vertical disposition of the axis that determines the *orthos* not only has an ethical and religious value, but also—and even prior to that—an ontological value. It is perhaps worth observing that, among the many iconic images able to perform the same function, the figure of the tree stands out because of its concreteness and simplicity. Whatever the generative power of the symbol might be, it remains inscribed in a general economy of signification that can rely on the analogy between the vertical development of the tree and man's erect posture. The vertical axis is precisely a structural premise for the productivity of the symbol—or, if you will, the order of verticality sustains and nourishes the entire structure.

It is evident that this structure is based on a geometrically organized spatial metaphor that contains an up, a down, a straight line, and sometimes even a left and a right [*destra*] (the latter symptomatically named as *dritta*, *droit*, *recht*, *derecha*, etc.). As often happens, the symbol's narrative efficacy consists not in the figure's abstract and stylized schema, but in its capacity to relate to a common experience—or, so to speak, to the empirical relation between man and tree (which is more than just visual). Counting on this efficacy, a minor Italian author of the seventeenth century, Angelo Paciuchelli, wrote a Christian moral text that can exemplify the whole question with particularly illuminating results.

> The symbol that explains man is called tree. "Homo est arbore inversa [Man is a reverse tree]," said Plato. "Video homines sicut arbores ambulantes [I see men that are walking around like trees]," said the blind man in the Gospels. Just like the Death's sickle has to cut the tree, and hence it will necessarily fall on one side or the other, either to the right of salvation, or to the left of damnation, and so will be forever. If you want to foresee on which side it will fall, observe on which side it inclines. If since youth it leans on the side of vice, it will fall into Hell, says St. Bernard.[5]

Paciuchelli concludes his discourse with the expected reprimands: "Oh sensual and mundane man, where do all your worries, thoughts, affections, plans, desires incline? Do they not lean toward sin? Toward Hell?" The spatial schema, which is intrinsic to his argument, is in fact simple and transparent: inclinations displace man from his vertical axis, making him lean to the left, hence destined for the sinister caves of Hell. For man, in perfect harmony with the nature of the tree, it is therefore prudent to grow well and keep straight. Within Christian morality, the subject's verticality, together with the tree's kindred botanical symbolism, function as a map to salvation: the erect posture, which functions as a model for moral rectitude, is a guarantee of Paradise.

As many experts maintain, the man-tree symbol is a "narrative icon" which, although it has a logic of its own, does not obey the rules of a rigorous apodicticity. Its various plots all suffer from paradox. Paciuchelli's text offers an example of this nonrigorous logic: he mixes realistic and unrealistic vocabularies with ease. Soon after his first scholarly citations, the author then proceeds to entrust the icon's efficacy to an image from ordinary experience, the cutting of a tree. Woodsmen and peasants, also ordinary people, know how it goes: cut at the base with an ax, the tree will fall where it leans. For Paciuchelli, the use of realism stops there. In the next passage, he changes register and argues that, if the tree is straight, it not only falls (oddly) to the right, but also vertically, so to speak, toward eternal salvation. Contrary to all empirical logic, in other words, on the right side there is no real inclination—only a fall that paradoxically is also an ascent. Put differently, as Paciuchelli's text shows in conformity with a long-standing moral tradition, inclination is always on the left, and is always sinful. The metaphorical man-tree, unlike the actual trees felled by loggers, thus only inclines toward one side. That the sinful side is on the left is not surprising: as a deviation from the vertical line, and hence too as an oblique pendency, inclination is structurally negative, a sinister omen of evil.

In fact, it is not even necessary to refer to obscure seventeenth-century Italian writers to retrieve the framework of this genre. Nor is it necessary to insist on the fact that religious treatises rely upon the tree's symbolic efficacy to evoke infernal punishments. Even a sober

Enlightenment philosopher such as Kant will speak of the "crooked timber of humanity,"[6] hence reinforcing another version of this tradition, whereby man is a crooked tree that needs to be straightened. The metaphor is ancient and, over the course of time, has succeeded in enlisting an army of rectifiers happy to lend their discipline to such a task. The crookedness of the soul: that's a project for philosophy and theology. Physical distortions, meanwhile, pertain to medicine and gymnastics. Pedagogy, for its part, not only has a fundamental role, but it also has an even larger domain. When old-time pedagogues used to say, "Stand up straight!" they understood themselves to propose a healthy physical posture as well as a moral admonition, if not also the formation of a truly virile character.

Around the mid-eighteenth century, precisely in Kant's time, the noble art of straightening up increased in importance and extended its reach to the capillaries. To speak in Foucauldian terms, the individual became the object of disparate techniques of rectification meant to straighten his posture.[7] Leafing through *Discipline and Punish*, one has the opportunity of admiring two illustrations from a book by the French doctor Nicole Andry, whose title sounds exemplary: *Orthopedics; or, The Art of Preventing and Correcting Deformities of the Body in Children* (1749). One of the illustrations features the programmatic Latin inscription "Haec est regula recti [This is the rule for straightness]." The other illustration shows a crooked tree secured to a straight pole with ropes. Andry is also the inventor of the term *orthopedics*, from the Greek *orthos* (straight) and *pais* (child). In young children as with young trees, the earlier the intervention, the more effective the straightening. In the age of Enlightenment, though, infancy was not the only developmental stage that preoccupied the specialists of postural rectifications. Destined to great success, the new discipline of orthopedics also had a larger significance. Looking closer, it selected as its motto a Latin phrase that could have been taken from the old juridical formula of "righting wrongs" [*raddrizzare i torti*].[8] It is not by chance that this formula can travel from the lexicon of the juridical to that of orthopedic science: straight is to right, as crooked is to wrong. The two fields share a geometric imaginary that is, for the

most part, arboreal. Crucially, as one sees in the etymological dictionaries of the Italian language, this is an imaginary that opposes *dritto*
("straight") and *diritto* ("right"), not only to *torto* ("wrong, twisted")
and *tortuoso* ("devious, crooked"), but also to *inclinato* ("inclined")
and *pendente* ("leaning, sloped, slanted").

Speaking of "straight" and "wrong," and taking a cue from Foucault, it is worth broadening this inquiry to include a brief mention
of recent developments in the analysis of sexuality. *Tortuous* derives
from the Latin *torquere* (to twist, bend), a concept that's also the root
for *queer*, through the German *quer* (oblique, transverse, diagonal).
In the Anglophone world, the term queer has become a pejorative for
male homosexuals. As Lorenzo Bernini observes, "'queer' is the opposite of 'straight' . . . since heterosexuality is traditionally associated
with moral rectitude, which is also, in turn, heterosexual."[9] In today's
slang, in fact, *straight* designates the heterosexual person, whether
man or woman, who loves the opposite sex and is therefore "normal."
The term *queer*, meanwhile, today designates not just male homo-
sexuality but also a wide range of identities and practices considered
deviant: gays, lesbians, transvestites, transsexuals, and other "abnormal" subjects. Much of the good fortune of the term queer is indeed
due to the rapid emergence of a school of thought that, not coinci-
dentally, goes by the name "queer theory," and which has submitted
to a radical deconstruction the normative framework that proposes
to define "normal" and "abnormal" sexuality. Thanks also to queer
theory, queer identities can be mobilized to denounce and above all to
contest the hegemony of the hierarchizing *dispositif* of heterosexuality that turns "right" and "straight" into synonyms. Here, in a certain
sense, the geometry of the vertical subject itself provides the basic
theoretical, linguistic, and political elements for its own subversion.
By empowering the oblique line and by turning the abject into a resource, queer theory challenges *Homo erectus* and consigns him to his
own "bad inclinations," which are "abnormal" and as a consequence
"unnatural."

Following an authoritative tradition, Kant categorizes homosex-
uality (*sexus homogenii*) among the sins of the flesh against nature

(*crimina carnis contra naturam*), together with onanism.[10] Kant appropriates this old thesis in the first chapter of his *Metaphysics of Morals* (1797), "Man's Duty to Himself as an Animal Being." As an animal or natural being, Kant writes, man has a sexual inclination the obvious purpose of which is "to preserve the species."[11] Even though man and woman may feel pleasure, they mate essentially for procreation, not for enjoyment. Outside of this frame, which juridically corresponds to marriage, sex is only a vice; even more when the vicious man performs sexual acts against nature, it is "a *defiling* (not merely a debasing) of the humanity in his own person."[12] The philosopher is quite clear on this point: "that such an unnatural use (and so misuse) of one's sexual attribute is a violation of duty *to oneself*, and indeed one contrary to morality in its highest degree, occurs to everyone immediately, with the thought of it, and stirs up an aversion to this thought to such an extent that it is considered indecent even to call this vice by its proper name."[13] This, Kant explains, is why men of this sort so often fail to call the vices by their true name. During the age of Enlightenment, which paid tribute to libertinism, Kant deployed all of his resources—from the rigor of the moral law to an unrestrained defense of sexually correct mores—to straighten the crooked timber of humanity. In his thought, *Homo erectus* found its inflexible champion. The need for vigilance was, after all, unending; the attacks, in this intellectually effervescent century, would come from many quarters. In Kant's time, in fact, there would even be a prestigious scientist who would declare erect posture itself to be contrary to nature.

6

We Are Not Monkeys

On Erect Posture

The chimpanzees are primarily visual
animals, but . . . they seem unable to
comprehend the vertical as the line
of gravitation; given their arboreal
existence, with its continually shifting
perceptual axes, this is not surprising.
Arnold Gehlen, *Man: His Nature*
and Place in the World

IN 1771, Kant wrote an ironic review of Pietro Moscati's *Delle cor-*
poree differenze essenziali, che passano fra la struttura de' bruti e la
umana (Of the Essential Physical Differences Between the Structure
of Beasts and of Humans), a speech the Italian doctor had given the
previous year in Pavia, where he was professor of anatomy.[1] In the text
in question—an academic lecture that Kant read in German translation—Moscati argued that nature had originally designed the species
homo as a quadruped or as quadrumanous. The erect posture, which
the species assumed thorough artifice and "hereditary habit," caused
numerous health issues. Verticalization, in fact, forced the internal or-
gans to dangle unnaturally, causing deformations and illnesses of all
kinds—or, in Moscati's colorful expression, "an Iliad of diseases!"[2] It is

helpful to specify that Moscati is not a precursor of Darwin, whose seminal books *The Origin of Species* (1859) and *The Descent of Man and Selection in Relation to Sex* (1871) were still a century away. His conception of man is instead consistent with his own epoch, which still understood itself in terms of the idea of the "great chain of being," a model of a closed and hierarchically organized cosmos in which all creatures are lined up according to their varying degrees of perfection—a *scala naturae* which is fixed and preordained, and in which man occupies the highest point. Moscati's rather daring thesis is that, within his assigned degree on the ladder, man overexerted himself and unfortunately abandoned his originary four-legged position for an erect posture. "The erect and perpendicular posture of man . . . is not a gift of the benevolent nature [but] is perhaps something man created himself."[3] Some men started walking erect and, appreciating the advantages but not foreseeing the damages, taught the posture to their children. This spread until, eventually, the whole human species inherited it. As for the damages—this is exactly what worries the Italian doctor. The fetus of the "biped mother," for example, is housed upside-down in the uterus for months, exposing its brain to a rush of blood which, in turn, predisposes humans to vertigo, apoplectic shock, and insanity.[4] In the lower grades of beings, by contrast, the quadruped animals that remained true to their natural posture have avoided such nuisances and diseases. It is worth repeating that Moscati doesn't think that humans evolved from animals; nor does he suppose the existence of a half-race of quadrumanous apes. He simply thinks that humanity's transformation from quadruped to biped was artificial, and that whatever well-known advantages it has brought, it also has caused serious damage. As a professor of comparative anatomy, and also as a doctor, Moscati thus registers his regret.

None of this convinces Kant, who is both amused and irritated by the bizarre idea of a human quadruped. Moscati's theory disturbs Kant for two reasons: not only does Moscati describe the erect posture as a disgrace, but he also thinks that human reason is the cause of so much misery. "Dr. Moscati proves that the upright gait of the human being is contrived and against nature," Kant observes; according to this "astute and philosophical" Italian anatomist, the human being was "enticed by reason and imitation to deviate from the first, animal set-up."[5] The philosopher of Königsberg, as one may imagine, does not appreciate the eccentric hypotheses provided by human zoology. For him, as for his contemporaries, man obviously was a biped from the outset. He has always stood on his feet and has always been erect—just like Barnett Newman's Adam. The first aim of Kant's review is thus to mock a scientifically preposterous "curiosity." In his brief review of Moscati, which is more than a simple defense of upright posture, Kant derides the empirical sciences because they waste time with unimportant details (even though Kant himself would face the topic of race in his essays "Of the Different Races of Human Beings" and "Universal Natural History of Man and Theory of Heavens").[6] He does not hide his annoyance with a discourse that focuses on the morphological analogies between man and animals, or even worse on the contrast between a benevolent nature and man's malevolent reason. In many ways, as Kant reveals at the beginning of his review, behind his criticism of Moscati lies a polite disagreement with Rousseau: the playful hypothesis that concludes the review is an explicit homage to the Genevan philosopher. Besides seeing to it that man, as an animal, had the healthy posture of a quadruped, provident nature also "placed in him a germ of reason through which, if the latter develops, he is destined *for society*, and by means of which he assumes the most suitable position for society, viz., the *two-footed* one."[7] In this way, Kant concludes, man "gains, on the one side, infinitely much over the animals, but he also has to live with the discomforts which result for him from the fact that he has raised his head so proudly above his old comrades."[8] The tone is certainly playful, but it nevertheless gives a glimpse of Kant's serious intolerance for the myopia of a discursive register that reduces human verticality to a mere empirical characteristic of the erect posture. Plato already had made a joke about this same topic, when in the classifications of *The Statesman*, he defined man as a biped animal, unfeathered and without horns.[9] Philosophers know how to take a joke, and are not above the joys of jests, but above all they know that man stands up and verticalizes himself in many different ways: by standing up on his feet, moving above beasts or even above his own species, raising himself toward the Most High, straightening himself up thanks to correct reason. He may even, as Kant assures, rise above himself. In the history of philosophy, the rich potential of verticalizing geometry takes many different shapes and assumes a variety of forms. Kant, adding to the list, offers his own contribution. But he finds it quite tasteless that, in such a complex and respected affair, the *homo philosophicus* and the *Homo erectus* should appear together as two faces of the same coin. Happy to occupy himself with purely spiritual erections, Kant found the time in 1785 to write another review of a text debating the problem of the erect stance. This time the text was by German philosopher Johann Gottfried Herder, Kant's former student who had veered toward Romanticism. Kant's review is broad and diverse, but relentlessly sarcastic.

"The human being is the first of creation to be *set free*: he stands erect,"[10] Herder observes enthusiastically. Herder's delight for the exclusivity of the human's vertical posture, which he expresses in the most exaggerated tones, is a distinctive trait of his writing style in *Ideas for the Philosophy of the History of Humanity*, the multivolume work he started in 1784.[11] Here he writes that, "as the flower stood there, in its upright posture closing off the realm of the subterranean, inert inanimate creation, to enjoy the coming of life in the face of the sun, the human being stands once more erect above all those bent to the earth."[12] He also claims that "by attaining erect posture, the human being acquired free and sensitive hands, tools for the most delicate of operations and a ceaseless groping for new and clear ideas."[13] As one can tell from this last citation, Herder's thesis is quite radical: not just language, but reason itself, is an exquisitely human characteristic, which owes its origin to the other special characteristic, the vertical posture. The reader, however, should not allow herself to be overly impressed by his flowing, Romantic language: his inspiration comes primarily from zoology.

In fact, as Kant says, the portion of Herder's work that he is reviewing "contains only the presentation of the human being as an animal in the universal system of nature."[14] Here, too, the schema of the *scala naturae* dominates his thought. Even though Herder is often considered one of the fathers of modern anthropology, he is (like Moscati) not a precursor of Darwin. Darwin himself, when he credits "an extraordinary amount of modification" to the erect posture and brain development, hastens to add that the human "is but one of several exceptional forms of Primates."[15] Herder, by contrast, exalts the divine privilege of man, and keeps man on a grade that is distinct from the ape. The human body, according to Kant's paraphrase of Herder, was built by God's hand on a certain conformity, "through the forming of the head for the *erect shape*, through inner and outer organization toward a perpendicular center of gravity."[16] The ape's head, in contrast, "was formed under a different angle and was not made for an erect gait."[17] Even though Herder reassures his reader about the distinction between man and ape, and even though he clearly leans toward the originarity and specificity of the erect posture, Kant nevertheless does not embrace his thesis.

In his review, with his usual irony, the philosopher of Königsberg notes that, first of all, to base man's rational faculty on the figure of erect posture means to "grope about on the guiding thread of physiology or fly in the air with those of metaphysics."[18] Even though he considers plausible the notion that man was given an erect posture "because he was destined for reason," Kant thus disputes Herder's more radical thesis according to which "he obtained reason through the erect posture, as the natural effect of the very same arrangement which was needed merely for letting him walk upright."[19] Herder's biological determinism troubles Kant, for whom the vertical posture is prudentially connected to rationality but is not its cause; Herder's tone, meanwhile, is too emphatic for Kant's austere taste, and Kant finds it unsupportable. In his review, Kant thus cites numerous passages from Herder in order to ridicule him: "Let us with thankful glance pause to admire this holy work of art, the beneficence through which our kind became human kind, because we see what new organization of forces begins in the erect shape of humanity, and how through it alone the human being became a human being!"[20] Among the finest fruits of the erect posture of man, according to Herder, are "the rule of justice and truth . . . peaceableness, sexual love, sympathy, maternal love."[21] Religion is also among those achievements: after having defined it as something unattainable for the "stooped animal,"

Herder adds that religion is "the highest humanity."[22] By giving man an erect posture, "God raised the human being up, so that he, even without knowing and willing it, would scrutinize the causes of things and find thee, thou great connection of all things!"[23] The vertical line thus functions as the pillar of Herder's thought: it is as important for his construction of a natural anthropology as it is for his construction of the essential relationship between man, God, and the cosmos. Herder, in other words, inscribes both "nature" and "culture" in an ontology of verticality that repeats itself on many planes, and hence functions as the principle and substance of his system.

Kant, for his part, offers an homage to the astrological paradigm that belongs to the same type of ontology. "Two things fill the mind with ever new and increasing admiration and reverence, the more often and more steadily one reflects on them: *the starry heavens above me and the moral law within me,*" he wrote in one of his most famous texts.[24] Taken from the brief "Conclusion" of the *Critique of Practical Reason,* this sentence has today become proverbial. It also has the merit of synthesizing Kant's ontology of verticality. "I see them before me," Kant says of the starry heavens and moral reason, "and connect them immediately with the consciousness of my existence."[25] These two things are for him, in other words, neither obscure nor transcendent, but instead transparent and incontrovertible. Put differently, the spectacle of the starry heavens reveals the creature to be a simple point in the universe, something insignificant in the sensible world. The ethical imperative intrinsic to the noumenal self, Kant writes, "infinitely raises my worth as an *intelligence* by my personality, in which the moral law reveals to me a life independent of animality and even of the whole sensible world."[26] Each of these two worlds, it follows, has its own type of verticality, the first physical and set upon the axis that raises itself from the earth to the sky, and that symptomatically conforms to the characteristics of the human's erect posture. The second, meanwhile, coincides with the autonomy of a free and rational individual who, by freeing himself from the world, proudly raises himself over himself.

7

Hobbes and the Macroanthropos

Humans are inescapably subject to vertical
tensions, in all periods and cultural areas.
Peter Sloterdijk,
You Must Change Your Life

THE FIGURE OF THE KANTIAN SELF, which proudly straightens itself up to celebrate the subject's autonomy, is but the modern variant, secularized and excessively austere, of a general system of verticality that traverses the entire history of philosophy, and that, depending on the epoch in question, assumes different configurations. In the ancient Greek world, the paradigmatic figure is the Platonic philosopher who verticalizes himself on the axis of the Good. The figure conforms to a conception of space whereby that which is above functions as a pole of attraction, as a principle that orders and empowers ascent. Making allowances for all due differences, a similar schema is part of the Christian tradition, where the place of the Most High and the cause of Ascension are reserved solely for God the Creator. Thanks largely to its codification in theological terms, the meaning of verticality in the western vocabulary both expanded and acquired greater precision. In the eleventh century, the works of Anselm of Canterbury played a significant role in this process. Besides making the concept of *rectitude* basic to his theological reflection, Anselm proposed a substantial equation between rectitude, justice, beatitude, and truth. God, the creator of the *rectus order*, is for Anselm both the *Summa Veritas* and the *Summa Rectitudo*, the highest point in the ascent of man—the point toward which man straightens his soul with all his strength through "an exercise of spiritual rectification."[1] In order to gain a sense of the extraordinary productivity of Christian language regarding the concept of *rectitudo*, however, it is necessary to turn to the great Augustine of Hippo, who already had established its basic formulas in the fifth century. In his commentary on Augustine's *De libero arbitrio* (On Free Choice of the Will), Robert Pouchet provides a valuable summary that deserves to be quoted in full. For Augustine, Pouchet writes: "The good deed, *recte factum*, leads to the right path, *recta via*; the latter is dictated by the correct reason, *recta ratio*, which itself refers to the sovereign Wisdom, which is God, author of the right order, *ordo rectus*, according to whom man's superior faculties must dominate his inferior drives; from this train of concepts derives the expression *recte velle*, probably from Seneca."[2]

It is worth noting that, in relation to the evolution of the vertical system, of all the expressions Pouchet mentions, it is the *recte velle* (or, if you will, the *recta voluntas*) that assumes a major role. In terms of the history of philosophy, if not of the history of ideas, the category of will itself is indeed, theoretically speaking, a novelty born in the Christian world. According to Arendt, "the faculty of the Will was unknown to Greek Antiquity and was discovered as a result of experiences about which we hear next to nothing before the first century of the Christian era."[3] Augustine, whom Arendt defines as "the first philosopher of will,"[4] had the merit of giving a speculative form to Paul of Tarsus's discovery that the will, fatally, is a spiritual organ characterized by an inner conflict with the inclination "of the flesh," which opposes it with internal resistance. The idea of *recta voluntas*, formulated by Seneca though it may have been, is thus actually born with Christianity—or more precisely, with Paul, whose points of reference are faith in Christ and the phenomenology of sin. Indeed, *recta ratio* has an origin that differs from its roots in Greek philosophy. Reduced to its essential drama, the plot begins with the *orthos logos* that appears sporadically in Plato but that finds a stable form in the writings of Aristotle, which the Stoics then made into the founding principle of the whole cosmos, establishing a crucial analogy, if not also identity, between human reason and both divine and natural law. In the Latinate world, the syntagm *orthos logos* would reach Cicero, who would render it using the expression *recta ratio*, in which form it would arrive first in Augustine and then in Thomas Aquinas, whose Aristotelian vocabulary would further reinforce it, ultimately delivering it definitively to the philosophical lexicon as "right reason," which today remains in use even if it sounds a bit dated. Although *recta ratio* and *recta voluntas* converge in the Augustinian codification of the vertical system, in other words, they nevertheless do not develop according to parallel histories. The *recta voluntas* has a more recent birth, even if it would be destined to generate fortunate progeny: within Christian philosophy, it cross-breeds semantically with the more ancient *recta ratio*, and, further back, with the *orthos logos*. As for fortunate descendants, it should be noted that at least one of the modern metamorphoses of the category of *voluntas* is the Kantian self, which verticalizes itself on the axis of its autonomous will. With the work of Augustine, however, we are obviously still only at the very beginning of the story we are tracking, not to mention in a very different context: far from coinciding with individual autonomy, the doctrine of *recta voluntas* needs the gift of divine grace in order to secure eternal life. Reprising the Pauline thesis of the hereditary quality of original sin, and insisting on man's inclination toward vice as a consequence of the fall (*ad malum inclination*, according to the updated text of the Catechism of the Catholic Church that remains in force), Augustine sees the inclination toward evil as a perversion of the right will, as a fatal deviation from the *rectus ordo* that, in conformity to the design of the creation, originarily raised Adam up toward God. It is only grace that can save Adam's children, thus rectifying the trajectory that, without God's intervention, would destine them to the fall and to eternal damnation. Augustine, like Paul, is notoriously pessimistic.

Thomas Aquinas, the major inspiration of the optimistic side of Christian anthropology, also insists on the lexicon of verticality upon which Augustine expanded, but in a very different way. This difference is plain from, among other things, the ambivalent usage of the term *inclination* in Thomas's writings: for Thomas, man naturally inclines toward the good because his natural inclination, far from tending toward evil as it does in Augustine, instead leads him toward the right path, the *recta via*. Citing Augustine, Thomas confirms that "when the will is sound [*recta*], its love is good; when it is perverted, its love is evil,"[5] which also confirms the general design in which the identity between *recta voluntas* and the good corresponds to the identity between *perversa voluntas* and evil. Unlike Augustine, Thomas does not think that the perverted will, springing from the original sin, has penetrated human nature and necessarily inclines all humanity to vice. He instead holds that, in the complex design of Creation, human nature is endowed with reason and is constitutively characterized by a *recta voluntas*: in essence, according to Aquinas, man need only follow his natural inclination in order to act rightly. The result is a complication in the harmony of the imaginary space that underlies the system of verticality. Paradoxically, in short, we encounter here a man who is naturally inclined on the originary axis of right, and who "ascends" in the right way because he indulges his natural inclination to the good. Here, in other words, right and inclination—rectitude and proclivity—continuously overlap and ultimately will even directly coincide.

Speaking of falls, on which topic he is undoubtedly an expert, Augustine writes in his *De libero arbitrio* that, while the stone's movement from up to down is natural and thus above criticism, the inclination of man's soul is voluntary, explaining why it is that "we charge the mind with sin when we find it guilty of abandoning higher goods to put lower goods first for its enjoyment."[6] This argument nicely exemplifies the complexity, even the aporetic quality, of Augustine's views on will. It is also interesting because the comparison between the stone's movement and that of the human soul appears in a famous passage by Hobbes, who reaches an altogether different "moral" conclusion. The passage is in *De cive*, where Hobbes illustrates the typically human *voluntas laedendi* ("will to hurt") that leads men to kill each other to preserve their own lives: in Hobbes's view, this dynamic is neither absurd nor despicable because it happens "by a real necessity of nature as powerful as that by which a stone falls downward."[7] For Hobbes, in other words, the human inclination to violence has the same "scientific" and "objective" status as the law of gravity. It is also worth noting that, far from assuming the role of a technical term, the term *will* in Hobbes's lexicon is interchangeable with a set of other terms, including inclination, desire, and appetite. As pessimistic as Augustine but more bloody, Hobbesian anthropology is characterized by a horizontality on which violent and congenitally "warped" individuals move and clash. This predicament explains the need for an omnipotent and terrible vertical political sovereignty to rectify these otherwise warped individuals. The general system of verticality, now in its most perfect political version, replaces the Christian God with a mortal god that, upright and threatening, dominates its subjects through terror.

Unsurprisingly, the political orders imagined by philosophers are for the most part marked by a verticality that organizes the structure of politics and constitutes itself as its generative and founding axis. With a few exceptions—ancient democracy or, even more, the anarchist formula that focuses on absolute horizontality—the geometry of political models, as a rule, develops vertically: according to the classical principle of hierarchy, it varies from drastic apical forms, to the figure of a pyramid, to other similar shapes. Case in point is the openly antidemocratic model of Plato's *Republic*, which insists upon the analogy between the *polis* as "man *writ large*" and man as "*polis* in a small scale."[8] In the design that creates a correspondence between macroanthropos and microanthropos, the centrality of the vertical axis is a structural topographic and hermeneutic principle: the soul's noetic part, and hence too the philosophers-guardians, stand near the sun of the Good, at the summit of the straight line, whereas the soul's other parts, and hence too the other "classes" of the polis, take their place on a lower level, according to the degree and function of each. As Plato argues, this arrangement is good and right—better still, it is the very operation of justice itself, because in the totality of man and polis structured by natural subordination, all parts share "to each his own." Notoriously, the image of the sphere has an important part in

this mechanism that Plato calls "harmonic," as revealed by the cos-
mological frame of the celestial spheres Plato describes at the close of
the *Republic*. The metaphor of the human body, which Plato evokes to
illustrate the tripartite division (head, heart, stomach) confirms that
it is *Homo erectus* who functions as the principal referent of political
design. Or, better, it is the *philosophus erectus* who emerges from the
Platonic process of verticalization. The allegory of the cave, remem-
ber, shows that he who stands erect on the perpendicular axis of the
truth, and who thereby turns his posture into the very principle of political order, is not simply a man but is more precisely a philosopher,
the new champion of human nature—in short, Plato himself. In the
analogy between microanthropos and macroanthropos, the vertical
dispositif of the *anthropos* is built on his theoretical erection.

Symptomatically, when political modernity searches for its theoretical foundations, a gigantic macroanthropos will reappear on the cover
of Hobbes's *Leviathan* (see Figure 4). The analogy between "large-scale
man" and "small-scale man" is, in this case, even more explicit. The
Leviathan comes into being, Hobbes writes, through the imitation of
that masterpiece of nature that is man: "For by art is created that great
LEVIATHAN called a COMMONWEALTH, or STATE (in Latin, CIVITAS),
which is but an artificial man, though of greater stature and strength
than the natural, for whose protection and defence it was intended."[9]
In the illustration of the frontispiece, the giant stands straight, threatening and terrible. On the surface of his skin, as if they were the scales
of the marine monster from which he takes his name, appear myriad
"small" men whom he literally incorporates. Straightened up by the
sovereign verticality that absorbs them, they finally have the chance
to rectify themselves and thence to live in peace. The Leviathan, in
other words, saves them from the "will to hurt"—literally, to wound,
hit, and ultimately kill one another—which is, according to Hobbes,
man's natural inclination.

"I put for a general inclination of all mankind, a perpetuall and
restlesse desire of Power after power, that ceaseth only in Death."[10]
This is, notoriously, the disastrous inclination that leads to the "war
of all against all." In the so-called state of nature, the Hobbesian indi-

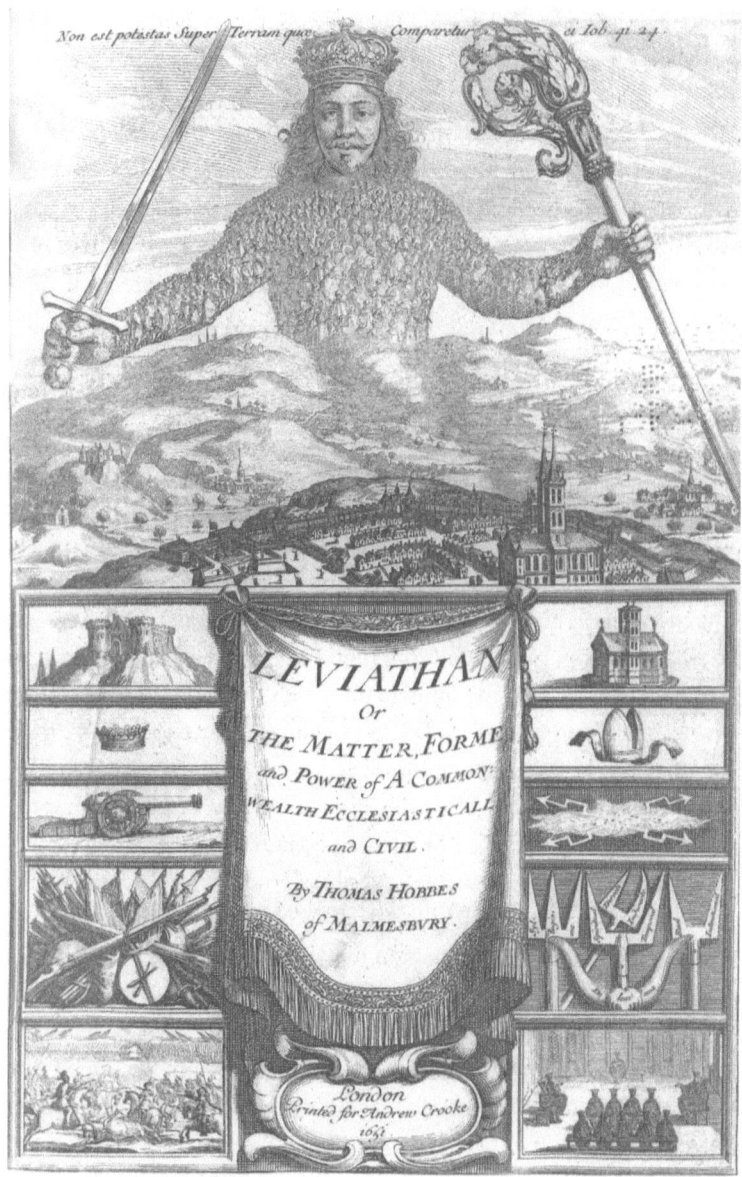

Figure 4. Frontispiece to the first edition of Thomas Hobbes's *Leviathan* (London: Crooke, 1651). Source: Wikimedia Commons.

vidual holds the originary right "to make . . . every effort to defend his body and limbs from death and to preserve them."[11] Homicide is the most effective of these endeavors. For Hobbes, in the state of nature, killing is not a crime but the result of life itself, understood as the blind and unstoppable mechanism of power [*potenza*]. In Hobbes's anthropology as well as in his political model, homicide thus has a fundamental role: besides functioning as an automatic defense for the natural mechanism of self-preservation, it also operates as logical criterion to found a political category—equality—that modernity cannot do without. Many have insisted, with a certain outrage, on the aggressive, competitive, destructive—in a word, violent—character of the individualistic paradigm Hobbes inaugurated. Few insist enough, however, on the role assumed by homicide in Hobbes's formulation of equality. "Those who have equal power against each other," Hobbes writes, "are equal; and those who have the greatest power, the power to kill, in fact have equal power."[12] The point of the application for this principle is the notorious "war of all against all," a paradoxical conflict that is perfectly horizontal and that can be understood only if one first grasps that the fighters on the battlefield are equal in their power to kill and to be killed. Life as continuously expanding power [*potenza*], in Hobbes's theory, produces its own speculative opposite: the absolute impotence of death. It should be remembered that the death in question here is not a natural death, the tragic inevitability of which has always served as a source of reflection for philosophy (metaphysics in particular). The death Hobbes has in mind is a violent death—that which every man may give to, or receive from, every other man. It is just this paradoxical scenario that ensures that men will decide to exit the state of nature and to create, by covenant, the great artificial man who, combining the forces of individual men into a single terrifying and irresistible power, is thereby able to ensure their peace and security.

"The Passions that encline men to Peace," Hobbes sensibly writes, "are Feare of Death; Desire of such things as are necessary to commodious living; and a Hope by their Industry to obtain them."[13] There is no contradiction between the feral natural man and the individual who, in search of peace, agrees to the pact that originates the State. The mechanism is, in each case, inclination—the natural drive and general product of selfish desire. The subject of Hobbesian anthropology does not then straighten itself up on the normativity of a vertical axis, as happens with Plato's philosopher and Kant's self. He is instead genetically bent by his passions—and hence too warped, unbalanced. Ceaselessly absorbed by forward movement, hungry for life and power [*potere*], he is always inclined in his motion. From a postural point of view, the majestic verticality of the sovereign that appears on the frontispiece of *Leviathan* does not correspond at all to the subject Hobbes theorizes therein. Or perhaps they correspond far too much: turning one's gaze to the international scene to consider the relations among States, one sees not only a renewal of the state of nature in the state of war, but also a transfer of inclination to the State. The gigantic *Homo erectus*, the State that ensures internal peace through the terror of its irresistible power, thus becomes a subject who, in relation to other States, is motivated by the same feral and violent logic of the natural individual. The Hobbesian phenomenology of power [*potere*] implies an inclination in the combatant that is both singular and general, regardless of whether their state is natural or artificial. In the end, therefore, nobody is perfectly upright. Though, as Weber says, the State may hold a monopoly over the legitimate use of violence, it nevertheless cannot escape the selfish and homicidal aggressivity that, according to Hobbes, constitutes its substance.

8

Elias Canetti

Upright Before the Dead

Here all theories come to a halt: they are
only used as means. Everything, through
simplification, is reduced to two images,
that of the standing man, and that of the
prostrate man.

Ernst Jünger, *The Gordian Knot*

IN THE HISTORY OF HUMANITY, understood as the history of in-
terspecies violence, the purest and most extreme form of violence
is described by Elias Canetti, with a bit of caricature, in a scene involving *Homo erectus*. Writing in the second half of the twentieth
century, Canetti depicts a situation in which a living man, standing on his feet, faces a dead man, who is lying horizontally on the
ground. "The living man never considers himself greater than when
confronted with the dead man, who is felled forever: at this moment,
the living man feels as though he had grown."[1] "The moment of survival is the moment of power. Horror at the sight of death turns into
satisfaction that it is someone else who is dead. The dead man lies on
the ground while the survivor stands. It is as though there had been
a fight and the one had struck down the other."[2] The second citation is from one of Canetti's major books, *Masse und Macht* (Crowds
and Power; 1960), from the chapter on the figure of the survivor;

the first is from a short essay in a 1972 collection called "Macht und Überleben" (Power and Survival).

The essay's title indicates the author's theoretical perspective, which inherits the realistic vein of Hobbesian anthropology, and which shows a special attention for a concept of power constructed on the blunt alternative between life and death. More than simply living, the individual Canetti describes is *surviving*—which is precisely to say that he is standing up in front of the dead man, "who never stands up again," and understands that "one is not dead oneself" but "one might have been."[3] "The confrontation with the dead man is a confrontation with one's own death."[4] This man not only wants to live; he wants to continue being there when others are no longer. The "passion for survival" is a specific trait of human nature[5]—as well as a straightening drive. For Canetti, in order for man to grasp the moment of the proud verticalization that realizes his will to survive, he needs to face the corpse's unchangeable horizontal position with his own erect posture. Constructed around the relation between those who lie down and those who stand up, Canetti's geometric imaginary is organized according to two elementary coordinates: the survivor's verticality and the horizontality of the dead. Although it is marked by a sinister elation, the framework here is clear—Cartesian and altogether simple.

Nevertheless, reference to the doctrine of Hobbes becomes inevitable, above all if one considers Canetti's emphasis on life understood as power [*potenza*], of which death is not only the direct negation, but also, according to Canetti, an occasion for the survivor to experience the greatest elation. To be sure, the power of life that pulsates in the Hobbesian individual inclines him to kill rather than causing him to stand up pridefully before the death of the other. For Hobbes, the rule of survival—the flip side of the *conatus essendi*—is killing. For Canetti, by contrast, killing has no decisive role; it represents only "the lowest form of survival."[6] The fundamental point, in this view, is not killing the other in self-defense or eliminating someone who is an obstacle to some vital desire; it is remaining alive while the other—any other whatsoever, as long as it is not himself—is dead. The scenario of Hobbesian anthropology is structurally a theater of war. Even if the combat amounts to a strange sort of war, one in which combat occurs not between armies but among individuals who act like wolves toward one another, the scene is nonetheless typical of bloody conflict: a general massacre is underway, and both the living and the dead are on the ground. In fact, because Hobbes's war scenario is perpetual, the living really should be called *morituri*, "those who are going to die."

Canetti, who came three centuries after Hobbes and lived through two world wars, calls them something different: "the survivors." Unlike Hobbes's natural individual, who is taken by the incessant movement of his desire for power, Canetti's survivor is a static figure, still, frozen in the moment of his supreme verticalization before the dead. Rather than struggling to preserve his life by any means—including, if need be, homicide—Canetti's survivor most of all enjoys an incomparable moment of triumph that crystallizes his erect posture. He enjoys his condition even when he should mask it out of politeness, cynicism, or convenience—such as, for example, during funerals or other sorrowful ceremonies. It is not by chance that Canetti identifies the battle—where the one who continues to lives rises vertically above the corpse stretched out at his feet—as the primal scene of the triumph over death. The author of "Power and Survival" was after all, writing during the second half of the twentieth century, in the wake of two deadly world wars. For the man of late modernity, in Canetti's works, "never is the standing man, for whom everything is still possible, more aware of his standing" than when he measures himself against a heap of corpses.[7] The fantasy of the state of nature has been surpassed by the actuality of mass wars that produce huge numbers of corpses. The act of reciprocal slaughter, so essential for Hobbesian political theory, has lost any sense: the only place that can produce sense, in any possible sense of the human qua human, is now the battlefield *after* the fight. Definitively encapsulated in his selfish verticality, when the survivor enjoys the moment of triumph over death, he also experiences an elating "sense of invulnerability."[8] "Something of the radiance of invulnerability," Canetti observes, "surrounds every man who comes back alive."[9] But the survivor's invulnerability shines above all in the moment of his confrontation with the dead who lie on the ground. The myth of the virile warrior and of homicidal violence still haunts the imaginary surrounding the human. But this is no longer a time for heroes.

In the history of the vertical subject's metamorphoses, Canetti deserves a special place, above all because his works provide an extreme figuration, which is almost caricatured and a bit grotesque. In the scene of the survivor who emphasizes his vertical posture in the face of the corpse, gloating about his own life in relation to the death of the other, what Hobbes's individualistic anthropology had announced is now completed. In a certain sense, by watching himself in the mirror of Canettian realism, *Homo erectus* meets the most cynical and selfishly sinister representation that his vertical posture had ever allowed him to imagine. It is precisely this pure and emphatic verticality, trembling but self-satisfied, that frees him from the austere ethical posture of the Kantian self, but also, more generally, from the moral vocabulary that traditionally has sustained the identity between straight posture and moral integrity (such as "rectitude," "straightness," "uprightness," or "correctness"). Canetti's survivor is undoubtedly straight, but he is also remarkably aloof from any moral precept that may attempt to define him as "just" and "right." Faced with the tangibility of death, "which one would like to call the only fact, and which is of such enormity that it takes in everything,"[10] the satisfaction of not being dead is enough to straighten him up.

Even though Canetti mainly considers the description of the survivor's posture, he is also interested in other postures, if not in the phenomenology of human postures in general. In addition to the substantial chapter on the "survivor" that appears in *Crowds and Power*, which Canetti would resume in his essay in "Power and Survival," there is also a special chapter in *Crowds and Power* dedicated to examining the various "human postures and their relation to power." Here the author broadens the spectrum of bodily postures, which in turn corresponds to a change of register: he puts aside the pathos of his theory of the survivor and assumes a colder analytical tone, noting that "the man who prides himself on standing upright can also while remaining in the same place sit, lie, squat, or kneel."[11] Canetti develops his inquiry both through a survey of the cultural and historical symbols in which ranks and power are associated with a "fixed, traditional pose" (as in the case of one who sits above all the others) and through a more abstract and original analysis of each posture in its own terms. He declares, in fact, that his main interest is to inquire into the specificities of each posture in isolation from its usual context: "A sitting or standing man makes an effect *as such*, irrespective of his spatial or temporal circumstances."[12] This historical-cultural perspective, typical of the anthropological register, encounters (without also absorbing) a theoretical perspective that clearly derives from philosophy's bad habit of posing the question of the subject in overly abstract terms. Indeed, in this chapter of *Crowds and Power*, Canetti speculates on man, understood in universal terms, maintaining that, for the individual, *being* on one's feet has a very different value from *being* on the ground. In other words, Canetti proposes an unusual framework: a treatment of postures that is really and truly systematic, that is no longer centered on the survivor's verticality, and that, as such, reframes the problem of the subject. Beyond the particularity and the complexity of the discourse Canetti develops here, there is therefore also a surprise: the meaning of the vertical postures now radically changes its sign.

In this system there emerges a different, perhaps even opposite, meaning of vertical posture than the one he developed in the chapter on the survivor. The implicit reference is no longer Hobbes and his violent anthropology, but Locke and maybe, with an even stronger influence, Kant. "Our pride in standing consists in feeling independent and needing no support," Canetti now writes; "a standing man feels confident and self-sufficient."[13] Gesturing to the lexicon of liberal individualism, the author mentions in passing "one of the most important and useful fictions in English life," in order to emphasize how "equality within a social group . . . is particularly stressed on occasions where all alike have or can have, the advantage of standing. No-one 'sits-above' anyone else."[14] Far from focusing on the sinister figure of the survivor, the scene Canetti now evokes almost coincides with an idyllic portrait of liberal democracy. The horizontal plane—guaranteed by an equality no longer founded on the will to kill but now on the universality

of reason—becomes the surface that allows for a dialogue among au-
tonomously vertical individuals. Here there is no hyperbole; the battle
is now fought through words, in a civilized way, and the dead exit the
scene. But make no mistake: Canetti's homage to the liberal version of
individualistic ontology is, aside from being superficial and cursory,
essentially ironic. Liberalism and its rituals do not belong to the most
authentic tones of the author of *Crowds and Power*. Whether ironic or
not, the ease with which Canetti shifts the meaning of the erect posture from the original theater of the battlefield to the liberal scenario
reveals the intrinsic adaptability that characterizes the geometry of the
vertical subject. It is worth repeating that in the history of philosophy
(if not in the whole western system, theology and politics included)
verticality assumes different configurations that codify in various
ways its elementary schema, sometimes to the point where multiple lines overlap on the same axis. Even just modern individualism
alone—understood as the expression of a determinate epoch, quite
apart from Hobbesian anomaly—allows for both of Canetti's versions:
the vitalistic and sinister one, as well as the more reassuring version
involving the free and autonomous individual who does not need to
see another's corpse in order to straighten himself up, with pride and
a touch of Kantianism, on the axis of reason. The latter version has inherited the vocabulary of *orthos* and *rectus* on which tradition insists.
This detail merits attention because philosophical texts typically do
not openly mention verticality, and because, unlike Barnett Newman,
philosophy does not avail itself of bars. Whoever goes in search of verticality needs to flush it out from the classic metaphors that conceal it.

Canetti, too, indulges in the art of concealment. If it is true that,
in principle, every system aspires to completeness, then it follows that
Canetti's system commits an important sin of omission: it doesn't
mention the inclined posture. Returning once again to Arendt, missing from Canetti is the figure of the inclination that disposes the subject along an oblique line, making it lean beyond its "natural" axis. At
first glance, this omission might appear negligible or perhaps, because
the object of Canetti's analysis is "human postures and their relation
to power," it might appear to be easily corrected by including cases in

which someone faces another and inclines his or her back or head. Philosophically, however, the omission takes on an altogether greater importance. Reconsidered with a bit of critical mischief, this omission in fact raises interesting considerations. One of these relates to the static nature of Canetti's array of postures, which distances itself from the Hobbesian individualism marked by incessant movement and a mechanics of inclination. The other question, more external and obvious, pertains to the absence of even the slightest mention of sexual difference in Canetti's analytics of posture. This is, of course, not entirely surprising, since Canetti's imaginary is inhabited by unmistakably masculine figures (such as the warrior who rises proudly erect over a corpse). What is surprising, however, is that such a fine writer, who otherwise is often quite capable of portraying splendid female characters, should remain so blatantly blind toward the figures of maternity, who traditionally are inclined. Here at least two important questions arise. The first concerns the possibility of relating the classic figures of feminine posture to a "content of power" that would justify inclusion in the Canettian schema. The second, more radical and indeed prerequisite, is whether it even would be possible for a figure of the human female to enter Canetti's schema of "human postures and their relation to power." For reasons we already have covered, having to do with the patriarchal tradition, this second scenario seems improbable. In the western canon, when the term "man" [*uomo*] appears in discursive contexts that thematize power, it tends to indicate a general category from which woman is programmatically absent. In this sense, Canetti is no exception. In his discussions of power, he only can see what his imaginary allows him to see: certain postures, but not others; certain warlike political scenarios but not domestic or more reassuring ones; images of death and terror but not those involving the fragility of birth. In the end, neither Canetti nor Hobbes is useful for rethinking the problem of inclination in terms that are altruistic and relational rather than selfish, aggressive, and violent. Should one wish to do so, a different path obviously will be necessary.

9

Artemisia

The *Allegory of Inclination*

One figure. A nude female. I want her to
represent Inclinazione, by that to mean his
natural talent. A quality you share with
il divino.

Susan Vreeland, *The Passion of Artemisia*

ON THE CEILING of the Buonarroti House in Florence, one can admire
Artemisia Gentileschi's beautiful canvas *Allegoria dell'inclinazione*
(Allegory of Inclination) (see Figure 5). A young woman, sitting on
a quilt of clouds, holds a compass with her hands. As if the woman's
body were attracted by a magnetic force, her naked bust and her head
of thick blond hair incline toward a small shining star in the painting's upper right corner. Commissioned by Michelangelo Buonarroti's
grandnephew in 1615 to honor the great Florentine artist, the allegory
represents inclination as a natural predisposition for art: artistic talent, Artemisia suggests, is like a lucky star that attracts artists and,
in a certain sense, irresistibly compels them to lean toward it. The
theme of astrological influence here takes the form of necessity: the
needle's compass cannot but succumb to its seduction by the Pole Star.
The compass and the star underline a fundamental aspect of the allegory: their arrangement along an oblique line signifies that artistic
inclination is subject to an *external* force, which prevents the subject

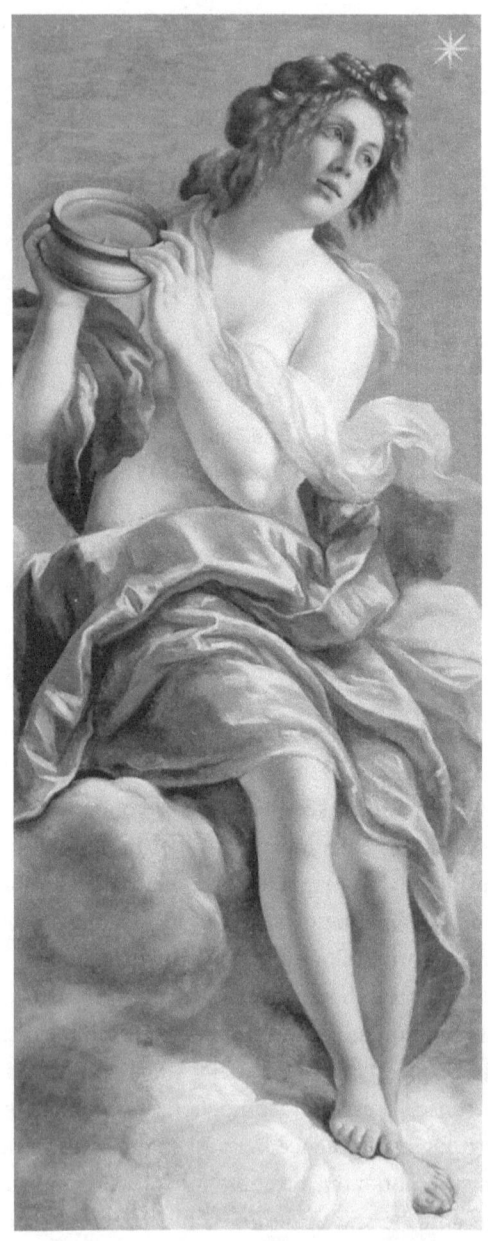

Figure 5. Artemisia Gentileschi, *Allegory of Inclination* (1615–16). Oil on canvas, 152 × 61 cm. Buonarroti House, Florence. Source: Wikimedia Commons.

from standing straight. This is why the usual firmness of vertical posture has no part in the experience of those who bend to art's pull. Even though the small star occupies only the painting's far corner, the whole composition is nonetheless obliquely oriented around its axis.

It is well known that Artemisia Gentileschi's paintings often contain elements of autobiography and self-portraiture. As for *Allegory of Inclination*, it is commonly believed that the young naked woman is Gentileschi herself, that the artist was a little over twenty, that she had already lived through the terrible experience of rape and of the shame of the ensuing trial that made her misfortune publicly known. Given such circumstances, her decision to use her own body for the naked portrait to adorn the ceiling of the Buonarroti's house appears as an act of courage and defiance. Her nudity soon would become the object of the sort of posthumous intervention that is all too common in the moralistic affairs of the history of art. A few decades later, another Buonarroti, feeling pangs of conscience, ordered a minor artist to touch up the naked figure, covering it with veils and drapes. The result is the figure who meets our gaze today and whose supplementary veils, by a curious turn of events, accentuate rather than chasten the exposed female body's splendid sensuality. Just like the great Michelangelo, to whom Artemisia wants to pay homage in this canvas commissioned by his nephew, Artemisia is herself an artist, subject to the same astral influence and the same inclination: she is attracted to painting, she knows her own talent, and she wants to show it. Unlike Michelangelo, however, she doesn't enjoy the approval of her society, which excluded women from art as from other intellectual activities. In a sense, Artemisia is naked because her pursuit of her talent isn't vested with any cultural authorization. Even more than Michelangelo, she is pure inclination: a female body attracted to, and bent by, the irresistible force of her artistic star. Or so it would seem, at least from this painting.

In a more mature phase, in 1639, Artemisia painted an oil canvas titled *Autoritratto come allegoria della pittura* (Self-Portrait as Allegory of Painting), which today hangs at the Kensington Palace in London. The painting shows a woman in an iridescent green dress, who inclines her body so that it stretches from her left arm, which appears in the lower left corner, and arches through the canvas until it then reaches her right arm, which holds the brush and rises toward the canvas's upper right corner, thus gesturing at the act of painting itself. As the main pole of attraction, the brush here replaces the star that appears in *Allegory of Inclination*. In the painting of 1639, as in the latter, a figure leans over an oblique axis on an empty monochromatic backdrop. Both canvases emphasize the attraction that is exerted by an object external to the person who makes it, drawing that person into conformity with a line of tension that at once inclines and raises the body. This is pure inclination: it moves from low to high, diagonally, toward the pole of attraction. Invoking the Muse at the opening of *The Iliad*, Homer already knew how artists seem to be moved by an external power, something that resides outside but is nonetheless irresistible and generates talent. Artemisia, though, should be recognized for having provided a visual representation that insists, almost didactically, on the translatability of this phenomenon into a precise postural geometry. Significantly, we here encounter the same imaginary that justifies the terrible reputation that human inclinations generally have among philosophers. Philosophers and artists judge inclination from different perspectives. Philosophers, convinced of the normativity of the straight axis, generally think that all inclinations, despite their variety, are basically malign or dangerous and hence in need of correction. Artists, meanwhile, thank their lucky stars for their inborn inclination to art, regarding it as admirable and constitutively benign. Artemisia is aware that artists are not the only ones convinced by this second thesis; the whole world, including even a large number of philosophers, in fact shares the same opinion. Crucially, this is one of the rare cases where the category of inclination acquires a positive significance: the miracle of talent rescues inclination from its usual negative frames.

We may clarify this question through a brief etymological digression. The term *inclination* derives from the Latin *inclinare*, which in turn derives from the Greek *klinein*: to bend, to be sloped, to lean. The Italian words for *decline* [*declivio*] and *bow* [*inchino*] share the same root, denoting a bending or curvature. The geometrical imaginary that gives these words their fundamental meaning is organized

precisely by the normativity of the vertical axis. Artemisia's painting provides a clear confirmation: if inclination can be allegorized
through an oblique body that traverses the canvas, it is because the
vertical line, or erect posture, provides the basic coordinates for the
whole framework. Artemisia exploits precisely the obviousness of the
straight line to insist emphatically on the oblique line's positive qualities. And, in fact, her emphasis is not misplaced, since her allegory
of artistic inclination was meant to celebrate Michelangelo's talent.
At a first glance, given the painting's subject, "inclination" and "talent" seem to overlap, or even to be synonyms. Artemisia obviously
knows that not all inclinations lead to true talent; but she also knows
well that when talent manifests itself in a great work of art, it testifies to a genuine inclination. All the same, it is blatantly false that the
term *talent*, as distinct from *inclination*, has a positive connotation.
In thirteenth-century Italian, the word *talento* clearly could carry the
definitely negative connotation of a weight that pushes down and
even crushes. For instance, in the famous fifth canto of the *Inferno*,
dedicated to Paolo and Francesca's punishment, Dante uses the term
to describe the inclination to lust. The dreadful circle hosts "i pecca-
tor carnali / che la ragion sommettono al talento [the carnal sinners
(. . .) / who make reason subject to desire],"[1] which is to say those
who let their appetites "sway their reason." The term appears in this
verse with a negative connotation that is completely authorized by
its etymological root, the Greek *talanton*, which indicates a "scale,"
"balance," or "weight." It is easy to guess how it later came to indicate an ancient coin, as some of today's currencies, such as the English
"pound" or the Spanish "peso" bear the same connotation. From the
idea of "weight," the language shifts to "coin" (which, in ancient times,
it was customary to weigh). Hence, the term can have the positive
meaning of "value" or the negative meaning of a force that pulls or
pushes down. The latter allows Dante to use the term to describe lust
(or, if you will, the attraction of the flesh). The sinners of the flesh
are inclined to sexual pleasure and are overwhelmed by the weight
of their desires that crushes even their reason, as the poet says. The
reason in question, it is worth pointing out, is right reason, or to use

a medieval term dear to Dante, *recta ratio*. Vertical lines continue to function as the norm. This verticality is the load-bearing axis against which one becomes able to "decide" the negative connotation of "talent" in the verse in question. For Dante and for the language of his time, the lemma for *talent* in fact preserves the originary structure of a meaning that Derrida would define as "undecidable." Its connection with the term *inclination* is a striking confirmation of this fact. Terms related to the phenomenology of "leaning" [*pendere*] and "imbalance," just like those related to inclination and talent, carry both positive and negative valences: it is the context that decides their meaning. In Artemisia's painting, the first one prevails; in Dante's universe, the second.

The presence of the astrological theme in Artemisia's painting reinforces the positive meaning of inclination understood as vocation, as a call to become an artist because of the stars' influence—because of an irrecusable election. As an ancient science of the stars, astrology establishes a connection between the position and movements of the planets and the character—the set of stable traits, the qualities or predispositions, and, in a certain sense, the destiny—of those who are born under a particular configuration of the stars. According to the immutable characterology of the astrological discipline, all human beings are uniquely defined by their inclinations. In the case of artists, one is often dominant: the Pole Star, as in the *Allegory of Inclination*, is said to attract, bend, and force the elected to art and to work. Michelangelo, like Artemisia, cannot escape this call: it is inscribed in the sky's eternal motion, having been fixed at the moment of his birth. In fact, the artist's inclination is at the origin not just of their talent but also of the world they create, which adds itself to the current world and tells of its beauty—and for some, even its truth. A close yet complex tie, indeed, traditionally holds art and creation together. The metaphor of painting as creative force fascinates even Plato, who is perhaps the harshest critic of artistic inclination and its illusory and deceptive products. Defined in the *Republic* as "painters of constitutions" (*politeion zoographoi*),[2] the philosophers themselves, after having dutifully erased the canvas, then will draw the most beautiful picture of the best polis, thus creating a form—a new world, an altogether different political reality—that was absent from the cave. The same philosophers are also, if not astrologers, then at least contemplators of the sky and experts in astronomy.

Apart from calls to art or talent, the most surprising lessons about possible links between inclination and the creation of worlds come from what is known as cosmology. In the history of philosophical cosmogonies, in fact, the first to incline itself is the atom. Or, more to the point, the world itself comes into being when atoms—which otherwise fall through a vacuum with inexorable, rectilinear motion—touch, thus subjecting their movement to a tiny swerve. The poet Lucretius, a follower of Epicurus and friend of the atomists, gave this inclination a name that would become renowned: *clinamen*.[3] The relation to the Greek verb *klino* is even more direct in this word choice. In the late imaginary of atomism, there is an originary matter that moves in a straight trajectory until it undergoes a deviation: the atoms' straight motion then experiences an inclination and assumes an oblique, and symptomatically life-bearing [*creatrice*], direction. The monotonous rain of indivisible particles, which otherwise would fall infinitely parallel to one another, now can open up to the adventure of a collision that is also a connection, a conjunction that is also a creation. For this atomism, in other words, inclination is at the same time relation and generation, which is what allows for the formation of visible things as composed by atoms, and thus too for the formation of the world itself. Without the *clinamen*, "nature would never have produced aught" says Lucretius.[4] "Only this deviation," Derrida comments, "can change the course of an imperturbable destination and an inflexible order"; only the inclination that "diverges from simple verticality" can interrupt the atoms' parallel fall and their mechanical fatality.[5] Very complex and rich with formidable philosophical and ontological questions, ancient atomism's originality of thought, especially in Lucretius's version, is striking. Often very bold in his thinking, Lucretius is also remarkable for his icastic statements, which notoriously leave their mark. "Nothing is created and nothing is destroyed," as Epicurus, for example, would repeat. For Epicurus, every thing is the temporary compound of immutable atoms that, by conjoining, bring the thing into being and remain after its destruction. Re-read with great interest by modern physics, the ancient atomists' doctrine probably goes back to Leucippus and then Democritus, a quite famous philosopher who lived in Athens during Plato's time. Indivisible, as their name suggests, and indestructible, the atoms are, for Democritus, elementary particles that form that varied and multiform universe we call the world. The manifestation of such a mixture, or the aggregative movement of atoms that produces it, needs another element to come into being: the void. However this is understood, it remains the atomistic doctrine's most interesting insight. Democritus's daring hypothesis on the genuine truth of the real—namely, that it is invisible and hence can be grasped only through thinking—employs a spatial and physico-geometrical imagery that eventually will provoke an unusual turning point in the history of philosophy. About one century later, Epicurus will inherit exactly this type of imaginary, along with the problem it implies: the fundamental question of movement and of the spatial configuration that allows for movement. For Epicurus, too, atoms move by falling from higher to lower points; but to the form given to atoms by Democritus, Epicurus now adds the element of weight. In his conception, atoms are heavy but impalpable: like raindrops on a windless day, they fall down infinitely along straight lines. The monotony of this scene is total and, for good reasons, despairing.

There is no other, no life, no sense. How would atoms aggregate, how would they ever meet, so long as their rectilinear motion forces them to fall only along parallel lines? So uniform and inhuman in its perfection, atomistic mechanics could continue forever without creating any world. It would remain a rain without land or sea, a rectilinear track with no beginning or end: pure necessity, desolation. Unless the *clinamen* intervenes—with its chain reaction of contacts and collisions that aggregates, forms, and creates. By interrupting the eternal fall of solitary atoms and by breaking the necessity of verticality, inclination generates the visible universe, both animate and inanimate things—the world. And, thanks to inclination, humanity itself can come to life, and begin.

10

Leonardo and Maternal Inclination

Children magically oblige us to incline our heads.

Ramòn Eder, *La vida ondulante*

LEONARDO DA VINCI'S oil painting *The Virgin and Child with St. Anne* (1503–19), which is preserved at the Louvre, is remarkable for Mary's posture (see Figure 6). She is at the center of the canvas, leaning forward, bent over her son, seated on the lap of her own mother, Anne. Anne, in turn, inclines her head slightly toward Mary, and also, following the axis of oblique gazes traversing the portrait, toward baby Jesus. Jesus, meanwhile, leans against his mother's leg, holding a lamb, a symbol of the passion and sacrifice that awaits him. The picture's invocation of the *vulnus*-to-come underlines the condition of vulnerability that Christ shares with humanity, capturing him in his infancy, that moment so exemplary of vulnerable defenselessness more generally. Leaning over baby Jesus, as if to spare him from his fate, the Virgin Mary holds his hand and body with an ordinary gesture of maternal care. Unbalanced along her own axis, she noticeably inclines herself.

Among the most admired of Leonardo's masterpieces, this picture has the merit of putting into particular relief Mary's inclined posture, if not inclination itself, as the geometrical matrix for the whole

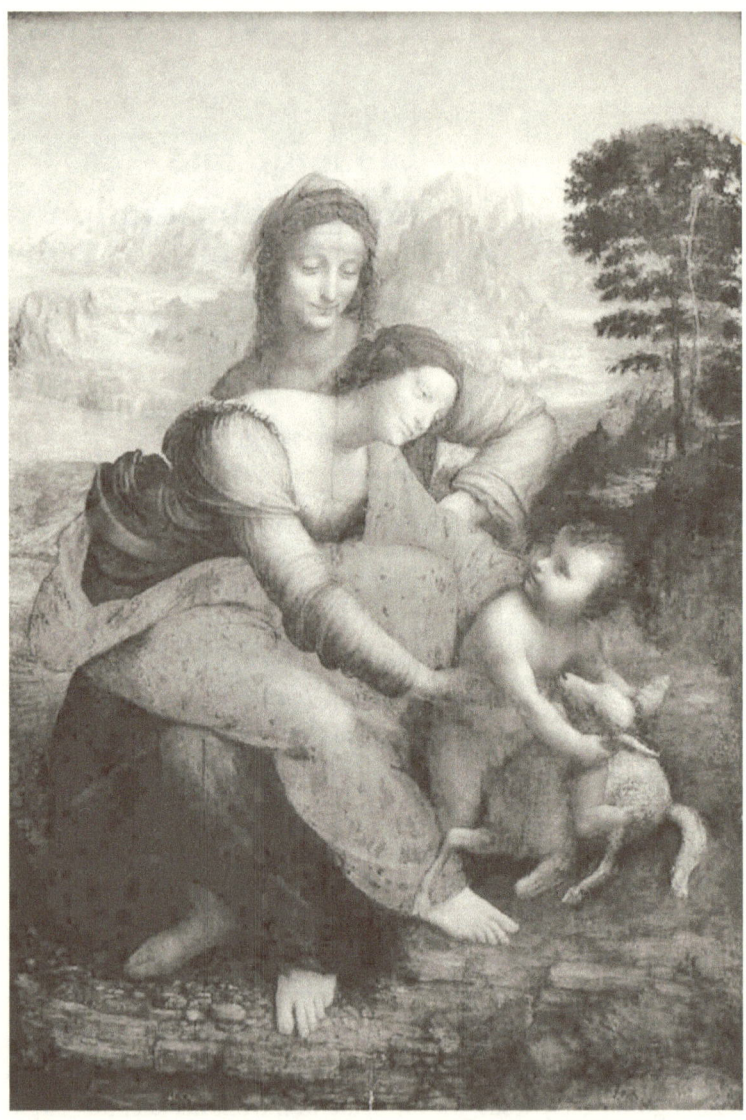

Figure 6. Leonardo da Vinci, *The Virgin and Child with St. Anne* (1503–19). Oil on poplar wood. Louvre, Paris. Source: Wikimedia Commons.

composition, while a straight tree in the background accentuates the effect. Confirming a subversive gesture originally performed in the *Virgin of the Rocks* (1483), Leonardo places the child beside the mother, and not in her arms, as in the traditional representations. In canonical paintings until Leonardo, the Christ child is not only held by Mary, but seated in her lap with his back turned to her, facing outward: according to the traditional canon, Mother and Child should not look at one another. According to these same standards, St. Anne's presence would have required the composition to have been structured as a vertical pyramid, with the three figures lined up, one over the other. Leonardo, by contrast, breaks with this system of symmetrical verticality, presenting a mother who is face to face with her child; a child whose head is twisted back to face the one who visibly tilts and stretches out to support him; and an Anne who observes them both with a smile. The asymmetry of this portrait, modulated as it is by inclination, translates nicely into the movement of a relationality that reflects the everyday experience of the maternal rather than the monumentality of the sacred. With Leonardo, the artistic process of humanizing the mother reaches its peak: his Virgin Mary has nothing of the hieratic immobility of Madonna Theotokos on her throne—nothing, in other words, of the Queen of Christianity who offers her son for the adoration of the faithful.[1] The mother here is inclined over her child who, as an emblem of dependent and vulnerable creature, attracts her in a forward motion, in a protrusion beside herself that endangers her balance.

If it is true, as Arendt thinks, that "every inclination turns outwards, it leans out of the self,"[2] bending us over objects or people, then Leonardo's painting gives the meaning of maternal inclination a special ethical density and a neat geometric linearity. Not only does it foreground the child's vulnerability and his dependence on others, but it also accentuates the relationship between Mary and her son, redoubling it through the relationship between Anne and Mary. The oblique line that traverses the painting is a matrilineal line; it gives expression to maternity's geometrical dimension, which is simultaneously temporal, projected onto a potentially infinite past. To prevent

Arendt's remark from causing misunderstanding, however, here a philological clarification is again necessary. Arendt's words appear in "Some Questions of Moral Philosophy," in the context of a reflection on Kant, in which she makes no specific mention of the problem of motherhood, much less that of maternal inclination. What is more, Arendt treats the category of inclination only occasionally, and in a way that doesn't really influence the analysis that follows. In search of a conceptual horizon whereby "the self and the intercourse between me and myself are no longer the ultimate criteria of conduct," her analysis recuperates certain features of Kant's aesthetic judgment, inscribing them, unexpectedly, in the field of ethics (on account of the fact that only in the context of aesthetics did Kant consider "men in the plural").[3] Even though the issue of the *other* is thus invoked by the Arendtian conception of plurality, the other—much less, again, maternal inclination—does not play a central role in the inquiry that Arendt develops. The question, as Judith Butler would say, is how to "dislodge the subject as the ground of ethics, only to recast the subject as a problem *for* ethics."[4] But Arendt's solution, however focused it may be on relational ontology in an anti-selfish key, nevertheless does not consider the figure of the mother.

And yet the maternal figure implies an immediate ethical tonality that a large part of feminist thought, with all manner of differences and hesitations, has never failed to emphasize. According to the most well-known literature on this theme, the maternal is understood as a primary instance of *care* for the *other*. The other in question, however, is not the other in general; still less is it the indefinite Other, looming with its enigmatic capital letter, that populates certain twentieth-century philosophies. It is instead the other who is held in the warm embrace—the son who is still a vulnerable and tender infant. And I do mean son, not daughter, because of the iconographic power, within western culture, of the Madonna and Child in the Nativity scene. Like all crucial figures in the symbolic order, the maternal lives in the intensity of its images and representations, which condense the concept in an exemplary way. It is certainly true that the stereotype of the self-sacrificing woman—a thorny problem for feminist critique—can count on the broad conspiracy of art and religion, which Leonardo inherits. In spite of its misogyny, the patriarchal tradition does not deny the feminine virtue of caring for others—to the contrary, it notoriously exalts it, especially when, as in this case, the interference of eros is out of the picture. The Virgin who appears as an icon of maternity is, in this sense, a very eloquent example. The woman who is called upon to express her "true" nature, or her authentic inclination, in the act of nurturing her child finds in the Virgin a reference that is at once unequivocal and paradoxical. A virgin, Mary also expresses the feminine as pure maternity. Because of a presumed congenital rationality (as tradition does not tire of repeating), the human male has a less paradoxical and above all less restricted range of expression. According to a schema that already is at work in Aristotle, man is meant *for himself* and for the political community, whereas woman, confined to the laborious domestic sphere, is meant *for the other*—which is to say, in the last analysis, for him.

From the very beginning, our inquiry has grappled methodologically with this repeatedly signaled and geometricized schema. Insistence on gender stereotypes is part of this method. Stereotypes—one could call them "frames of meaning," or, according to a certain feminist lexicon, "culturally constructed sexual identities"—are obviously difficult to dismantle. This is especially so with the stereotype of maternal inclination, particularly in its self-sacrificing role. And yet, among the aspects that recommend the maternal as an ethical paradigm, there is one that is often overlooked but that deserves attention: the scene of birth and, in particular, the ontological framework it offers to a philosophical tradition that is usually more preoccupied with death. The exception, of course, is precisely Hannah Arendt, who, commenting on natality as the fundamental condition for human existence, makes it coincide with the "the naked fact of our physical appearance."[5] The theoretical context in which this phrase appears—and this merits special attention—is a critique of metaphysics that rejects both the modern and ancient categories of "nature" in order to focus on the far less common category of "condition." The human being is in the world, observes Arendt: beginning with the crucial moment of our initial appearance, and lasting throughout our entire existence, the human being is constitutively exposed to others—which is also to say, above all, exposed to the mother, despite Arendt's reticence on this topic. Despite the richness of Arendt's discovery of the category of natality, it is especially necessary to include the mother in any scene of birth if we are to take full advantage of that category, particularly if the task is to liquidate the leading role of auto-referential self. Embodying the other in relation to the newborn over whom she leans, the mother not only confirms that scene's relational and antivertical character, but also, by predisposing it to an altruistic ethics, requires that it be understood in terms of dependence. It is worth repeating that the main problem is how to persuade the self, proudly encapsulated in its verticality, to renounce its claim to autonomy and independence. The newborn—the infant, the little child—thus becomes an ideal figure: when confronted with the primary roots of existence—with its natal condition—the transparent and self-referential subject typical of modernity falters and reveals all of its vanity. It is not by chance, after all, that this subject is the traditional subject of ethics. Wrapped in his narcissism—both morally and, prior to that, ontologically—the subject who is favored by philosophical tradition neither exposes itself nor leans out of itself. It instead aims at becoming immune to the other through an act of self-foundation and by pretending not to need the inclination of others. Disputing the immunitary paradigm of the self,[6] however, the infant not only exposes itself in a complete and irremediable manner; it also exhibits a congenital vulnerability as its fundamental constitution and condition. Already indebted to the *other*—the mother—for his arrival in and persistence within the world, the newborn depends, precisely by virtue of his vulnerability, on the one who, inclined and thus bent forward outside herself, leans over him. All the more so when it is emphasized, the posture of self-sacrificing maternity thus becomes a figure that can keep in check the vertical system in general and the verticalized subject in particular.

For this reason, the contraposition suggested by Carol Gilligan's *In a Different Voice*—between a feminine ethics of care and the masculine predisposition to formulate abstract moral judgments—is only a premise.[7] The same goes for the generic contrast between a relational ontology and an ontology that continues to be based on the individualist paradigm. Because it calls into question a relationality which is originally dual, and because it is characterized by a relation that is unequal and even unbalanced, the scene of natality is indeed more complex. First of all, there are two personas on stage in this scene: mother and child. If the former must protect against the well-known risk of sinking into the stereotype of self-sacrificing woman, the latter seems to call for precisely that self-sacrifice because of his position of extreme vulnerability. For the infant, in essence, this is a relation of dependency that is as crucial as it is unconscious and unidirectional; it is a complete passivity in the face of the acts, whether benign or malignant, performed by the one who inclines over him. In this respect, the infant—especially the newborn—embodies, in an exemplary way, the other as defenseless.[8] It does not matter here whether the infant is a boy or a girl: because it is an embodied singularity and not some fictitious entity contrived by metaphysics, the newborn always has a sex; but the vulnerability of the human condition it announces and incorporates in the extreme form of its defenselessness does not depend on sexual difference. The infant's vulnerability is independent from gender; it appears to be so imperative that one could extract a representation of universality from it, thus turning the infant into the plausible champion of the hyper-represented theater of maternity, It would be a mistake, however, if not also the effect of an old metaphysical vice, to suppose that the scene of natality can claim a total noninterference from sex. In the dual relationship that is under examination here, the *other*—rigorously gendered as woman—is always a part of the picture: even if she should happen to be replaced by another, the name of the imaginary mother remains in play. Generated by an infinite chain of she-others who are lost to humanity, she in turn generates vulnerable beings. Above all, and well beyond any act of procreation, she performs a role that can never be symbolically supplanted: she is the one who responds to *others*.

Following Arendt—who, in this, unexpectedly follows Hobbes[9]— we need to try to observe the scene of natality as distinct from the (likewise fundamental) event of childbirth. There are at least two reasons for a strategic move of this sort. The first derives from a justifiable suspicion of a tradition that, even in today's discourses on bioethics, tends to systematically conflate the maternal with gestation and procreation. The second, as explained above, pertains to Arendt's suggestion of an ontology that defines the human condition in terms of appearance. Warning us, among other things, that "there is always more at stake in life than the sustenance and procreation of individual living organisms,"[10] Arendt also seems to push us in precisely this direction. In Arendt's words, the human being is in fact an irremediably unique being, in that its belonging to the world entails its appearing to the world. In other words: not only is the one who appears *already there*, but there is also no preceding stage—let alone some embryonic state— that can influence the significance of its actual being-there, which is ontologically contextual, intraworldly, and material. In this sense, the newborn represents the most effective paradigm of the inseparable coincidence between existing and appearing. And, in the same way, even if in spite of Arendt, the mother is necessarily in the frame of this picture, but not by virtue of the title that is conferred upon her by the act of childbirth. Instead, she plays the role—as Leonardo's exemplary portrayal, as well as daily experience, attest—of the one who responds quintessentially to the infant's vulnerability, by leaning over him within the relational context. "Mother," it is worth repeating, is thus above all the *name* for an inclination toward the other—or, if you will, for a function that summons the requisite responsibility in the inaugural scene of a human condition in which the absolutely vulnerable—the defenseless—becomes an essential figure, first for ontology and politics, and then for ethics.[11] The infant, meanwhile, is a creature who is completely in the care of the other: infancy is an almost singular form of existence destined to turn itself into an unaware but peremptory solicitation. As such, the infant highlights the originary paradigm of human vulnerability: being defenseless, the infant is archetypal in a double sense, both because everybody's life begins with infancy, and because the principle of infancy returns whenever, in the course of life, one happens to find oneself defenseless.

To think the maternal merely as care, however, not only risks repeating the stereotype of the self-sacrificing woman; it also, and above
all, obscures the ethical valence of inclination, which consists in the
alternative between care and wound. And yet, even though it traces
a relational structure that frees the moral from the self's verticality to
focus on the other's vulnerability, the scene of the mother inclined over
the infant does not constitute a response either—only a disposition to
provide one. It is, indeed, just the act of leaning over the defenseless
creature and its unilateral exposure, which calls for it. In this sense, the
act of not inclining oneself—the act of remaining straight, of turning
around to leave—corresponds to an avoidance of the question, which
is to say, a refusal of a human condition that singularly interpellates us
insofar as we partake in the human condition. Avoidance of this sort
corresponds, in other words, to evil as an expression of irresponsibility, which is structurally distinct from evil understood instead as a violent act. The immense and moving literature on infant abandonment
feeds on the drama of such irresponsibility. It testifies to a prejudicial
form of violence, which can be deemed atrocious, but which is con-
ducted under the rubric of the inflexible and self-referential "I"—the
one who erects himself as if a vertical bar. The alternative between care
and wound, as well as that between love and violence, is by contrast
entirely inscribed in inclination as a predisposition to respond. Extro-
verted, stooped, responsive—this posture is typical of a self that bends
itself over the other, conspicuously abandoning its own balance.

As if the history of the imaginary knew what moral philosophy
ignores, each pole of the alternative between care and wound can
rely upon a powerful iconographic gallery. Alongside Leonardo's Madonna lovingly bent over baby Jesus, consider Euripides's Medea, the
infanticide. A scandalous figure, Medea reminds us that care is not an
automatic or obvious response of maternal inclination; it is instead
the ordinary and indeed desirable side of a violence that is rare and
therefore scandalous, but that nevertheless remains equally plausible, since the defenseless creature is by definition "vulnerable." The
"vulnerable creature" carries the *vulnus*, the wound, in its very name,
which seems to destabilize the ethical alternative, tilting toward the

side of the wound—or, if you like, toward a response that is afraid of evil because it recognizes its enormous power of attraction. This does not of course imply that maternal inclination leans toward infanticide instead of care, only that infanticide can be perceived over centuries as the most scandalous crime precisely because, by negating care in a contextual and direct way, it comes to confront care as the other side—indeed, the ordinary side—of ethical response. To lean over the infant is to lean over an other who is absolutely exposed to being wounded but who cannot wound in return. This relation is without reciprocity; it is structurally asymmetrical. Maternal inclination does not decide for good or evil; it simply bends over the infant, outlining a scene in which good and evil, care and wound, enacted with full and unilateral power, cannot contemplate any retaliation.

"In the thirteenth and fourteenth centuries," Luisa Accati writes, "the image of Anne holding Mary on her lap was especially successful in Italy, where they were joined by the Christ child. The three characters become even more popular during the fifteenth century."[12] The image of Anne with the young Mary on her lap blends with that of Mary holding the Christ child. In this way maternity is redoubled by the exclusion of fathers. In Leonardo's painting, which confirms the general system, the Virgin Mary sits on her mother's lap: Anne supports Mary, almost anchoring her, as if helping her to lean outside herself in her inclination for her child. Rather than holding Mary back, so that Christ would not be spared his sacrifice (in which case Mary would represent the Church), Anne instead allows her to bend. The image, in a sense, suggests that every mother has had a mother, following a potentially infinite series of unilateral inclinations that are first received and then given. Of this image, of course, we can see only a small portion: Jesus represents a part of it that is ideally its end but genealogically its limit. Perhaps by giving further meaning to the absence of Joachim and Joseph, the Leonardian version of the fatherless Holy Family lets the vulnerable one—precisely as a being destined to the *vulnus*—turn his eyes back to the theory of mothers.

11

Hannah Arendt

"A Child Has Been Born unto Us"

Birth is always and in all ways a *paso
doble*, an hendiadys. In birth—this unique
event, this originary scene—there are two:
what was one becomes two and one of the
two is always necessarily a woman.

Francesca Rigotti,
Giving Birth with Body and Mind

AT THE CLOSE OF THE DENSE CHAPTER on action in *The Human
Condition*, Hannah Arendt recalls a citation to great effect. In the
chapter, she had just reasoned that action, the political faculty par excellence, is "ontologically rooted" in the "fact of natality," and serves
as "an ever-present reminder that men, though they must die, are not
born in order to die but in order to begin."[1] To strengthen her argument, Arendt then compares action to the miracle:

> [The miracle] is, in other words, the birth of new men and the new
> beginning, the action they are capable of by virtue of being born.
> Only the full experience of this capacity can bestow upon human
> affairs faith and hope, those two essential characteristics of human
> existence which Greek antiquity ignored altogether. . . . It is this faith
> in and hope for the world that found perhaps its most glorious and

most succinct expression in the few words with which the Gospels announced their "glad tidings": "A child has been born unto us."[2]

The citation is suggestive but wrong. The Gospels, which announce with true joy the birth of the child, do not include the phrase "a child has been born unto us," which instead appears in the book of the prophet Isaiah (9:6), where it is translated into English with the formula "For to us a child is borne" (or, in the King James Bible, which is probably the source of Arendt's citation, "For unto us a child is born"). The error, if indeed it is an error, is therefore double: Arendt here refers a rough quote to the wrong source (the Gospels instead of Isaiah).[3] That Arendt often cited from memory, with rather imprecise results, is well known to her interpreters. In this case, however, her infidelity to the letter assumes a meaning that is far from banal. The prophetic text carries with it a messianic charge that would create many complications for the thesis that Arendt is illustrating here. The text of the Gospels, by contrast, is more susceptible to a secular reading, and as such places the fewest obstacles in the way of the Arendtian strategy of circumscribing the sense of birth to the ambit of the untranscendable horizon that, in her vocabulary, goes by the name of "the world." Since for Arendt "living" and "being among men" mean the same thing,[4] the child—indeed, every newborn, each human being who makes its entrance into the world—is not born *to us* coming from *elsewhere*, but instead, according to the Arendtian vision, appears *among* us *here*. Whatever the sacred text that exemplifies it, Arendt considers the scene of birth, like that of action, to be radically mundane scenes that do not involve any transcendence or instances of religious salvation. Jewish and secular, fond of the classical Greek and Latin in which she was trained, but with little familiarity with Hebrew or with Jewish tradition, Arendt became acquainted with Christian thought mainly through Augustine, to whom she dedicated her doctoral thesis ("Der Liebesbegriff bei Augustin" [The Concept of Love in Augustine]), which was published in Berlin in 1929), and who would remain a constant reference for her. One of Augustine's phrases—"initium ut esset homo creatus est"[5]—appears a bit obsessively and repetitively in connection with the concept of birth, not only in her dissertation, but also in later texts, including *The Human Condition*. In her monumental work *The Origins of Totalitarianism* (1951), which precedes *The Human Condition* by seven years, she already had written: "Beginning, before it becomes a historical event, is the supreme capacity of man; politically, it is identical with man's freedom. *Initium ut esset homo creatus est*, "that a beginning be made, man was created', said Augustine. This beginning is guaranteed by each new birth; it is indeed every man."[6]

In her inquiry into the somewhat philosophically anomalous problem of natality, Arendt will thus highlight two contributions from Christian tradition: the glad tidings that announce the coming of the child, and Augustine's commentary on the story of Creation.

For Arendt, the relation between birth and action is very close—so much so that in *The Human Condition* the one always refers to the other. In appearance, at least, it is birth that assumes the primary role and is established as the foundation for action. Because it functions as an ontological root for action, in fact, it cannot but present itself as a *primum logicum*. Defining natality as "the central category of political, as distinguished from metaphysical, thought,"[7] Arendt situates it as the fundamental condition for a singular existence that begins, and that action, as the capacity for beginning and for distinguishing oneself within plurality, inherits and re-creates. Even if it is cited in an erroneous way, Arendt's reference to "glad tidings" primarily has the task of alluding in an exemplary way to the everyday "miracle" that repeats itself in every birth—this moment when someone new, unique, and unrepeatable appears among us, this beginning marked by uniqueness, this human being at its inception. Arendt puts special emphasis on the *novelty* and *uniqueness* that the newborn—that every newborn—reveals to the world, which is to say, to others, to those around the newborn. These same characteristics, not surprisingly, are used by Arendt with the same emphasis when she defines the category of action, which includes acts and words, and its structural political relevance. In Arendt's anomalous vocabulary, it is worth recalling, the term *political* designates a relational space of reciprocal appearance generated by the words and deeds of a plurality of agents (or better, of "actors"). The salient characteristics of this space are novelty and uniqueness; because they make manifest "the absolute difference of all men from one another,"[8] they are an unmistakable expression of the human condition of plurality. Action is structurally connected with this plural dimension: in its absence, there would be neither politics nor humanity in the proper sense. Action is primarily the faculty to begin, to seize the initiative, to give life to the new; "its impulse springs from the beginning which came into the world when we were born and to which we respond by beginning something new on our own initiative."[9] It is also, at the same time, the specific mode in which, by appearing on a shared scene as both actors and spectators, human beings actively reveal their respective uniqueness by distinguishing themselves, rather than just differing from one another, thus revealing *who* they are. Through action, Arendt clarifies "we insert ourselves into the human world, and this insertion is like a second birth, in which we confirm and take upon ourselves the naked fact of our original physical appearance."[10] The emphasis on the human is not pleonastic. What is at stake in the interactive scene that actualizes the fact of natality and realizes the phenomenology of beginning, is not just the authentic form of politics in the Arendtian sense, but also the human itself: action and speech, she insists, are "the modes in which human beings appear to each other, not indeed as physical objects, but *qua* men."[11] "This appearance," she continues, "rests on initiative, but it is an initiative from which no human being can refrain and still be human."[12] For this reason, as Arendt says, we are born twice: first as newborns, and second (and then repeatedly thereafter) as "actors" on the political scene, confirming us as unique and, as it were, as beginners. The newborn thus, in a certain sense, reemerges in the agent—by exhibiting the status of the human condition in its inaugural scene, the newborn also constitutes the announcement and ontological premise of action. In speculative terms, this means that the newborn constitutes the foundation of action and thus too of politics.

On the same page of *The Human Condition* that closes with her citation from the Gospels, Arendt writes that "the life span of man running toward death would inevitably carry everything human to ruin and destruction if it were not for the faculty of interrupting it and beginning something new, a faculty which is inherent in action like an ever-present reminder that men, though they must die, are not born in order to die but in order to begin."[13]

This affirmation is interesting for at least two reasons. First, it reaffirms the radicality of Arendt's reversal of perspective from death to birth—which, to put it in her terms, means the transition from death as the central category of metaphysics to natality as the central category of politics. Second, it further tests this reversal of perspective by confronting it with a geometrical imaginary that enjoyed great success in the tradition of the ancients. This is the well-known imaginary that attributes to nature a circular movement, symbolized by the figure of the circle. Arendt observes in this respect that, "from the standpoint of nature, the rectilinear movement of man's lifespan between birth and death looks like a peculiar deviation from the common natural rule of cyclical movement."[14] In contrast to the circle, which is called upon to symbolize the immortal life of the species through successive generations, the mortal life of the individual assumes the form of the shortest line between two points, a path that runs straight to ruin, to the end, to disappearance—in short, to death, since "the most radical experience of disappearing is death, and withdrawal from appearances is dying."[15] If one were to substitute appearance for disappearance—or, more to the point, if one were to substitute birth instead of death as the preferred philosophical category—the pattern also would change. Birth, as Arendt understands it, is more than just the starting point for a straight line that is already rigidified by the inexorability of its path towards its endpoint. It is the beginning of a journey whose itinerary is not yet identified, the event of a possibility in its pure state; with respect to the cyclicality of nature, it is not a deviation but an interruption. In other words, if we confront the ancient figure of the circle with natality instead of with mortality, beginning comes to the foreground and, by breaking down the circularity of natural movement, resoundingly interrupts it. Thus it is that the newborn breaks out of the circle, together with the human faculty that corresponds to it and that actualizes its disruptive force—namely, action. One can thus understand why "the birth of new men and the new beginning, the action they are capable of by virtue of being born,"[16] can resemble a miracle. *A child has been born unto us*: for Arendt, this formulation refers precisely to the miracle that interrupts the natural cycle's monotony, a miracle that pertains to the dimension of immanence and contingency,[17] which paradoxically happens with punctual regularity in the moment of every birth. In Arendtian terms, there is nothing sacred or arcane in the condition of natality; because it escapes the circle's predictability, and because every human being came into this world through birth, it applies to all of us. There is rather the regular opening toward a horizon of meaning that tears singular existence from the law of necessity and defines the characteristics of a free being (namely, a capacity for action). From the newborn, one expects the new and unexpected, the unpredictable and the incalculable: not only does natality supplant the inexorability of death with the unpredictability of beginning, it also breaks with every automatism, so that the individual life can no longer be thought as a straight line running to ruin.

One of the most acute interpreters of Arendt's thought, Simona Forti, rightly notes that Arendt's "ontological rooting of free action in beginning, as represented by birth, is not always convincing."[18] Given that Arendt calls upon action, understood as a synonym for freedom and spontaneity, to redeem the human from the biological dimension that reduces the human to a mere "natural being," it is indeed a bit surprising that she should turn precisely to a natural phenomenon— birth—to constitute the foundation of action. This problem, among others, has been taken up in a meticulous essay by Miguel Vatter, who explicitly chooses to question the relation between birth and action in Arendtian thought in light of contemporary debates on biopolitics. Vatter's central thesis is that in *The Human Condition* and other concurrent writings, Arendt's category of natality has the role, above all, of "a biopolitical concept that counters the 'thanatopolitical' concept of bare life,"[19] which Arendt already had explored (albeit not in these same technical terms) in her chapter on the horror of the extermination camps in *The Origin of Totalitarianism*. That Arendt's analysis of the totalitarian universe anticipates the Foucauldian paradigm of biopolitics (or even, in fact, constitutes an original version of it) is, of course, a point on which many interpreters today agree.[20] Vatter, however, expands the argument, arguing that natality too is a biopolitical concept, albeit one that is positive by contrast. According to Vatter, Arendt initially identified the lager as an atrocious factory that, by manufacturing men who were reduced to automatons, or "transformed into specimens of the human animal 'man,'"[21] destroyed the givenness of human plurality. Arendt then employed natality, Vatter contends, as a category able to biologically found plurality itself: "natality, by giving birth to singulars, is the freedom of biological life."[22] In sum, according to this reading, Arendt's concept of birth responds to a need, throughout the development of her thought, to connect human freedom to life, and thus too to a biological condition. Articulated through demanding textual comparisons, Vatter's thesis is interesting but perhaps too daring. Even though Arendt's account of the relation between birth and action presents many problematic or unconvincing aspects, her conception of politics—precisely where "glad tidings" become the emblem of her argument—seems to mobilize a theoretical framework that the lexicon of the biological language really struggles to contain. As Vatter himself laments, Arendt moreover never dedicated herself to a thorough analysis of the concept of natality, either from the side of biological life or from the side of Augustine's theology and creationism. Natality is, in other words, a fundamental category that Arendt herself does not define with precision. In fact, one could even argue that, in Arendt's peculiar vision of politics, birth remains a greatly innovative, decisive, and surprising concept that is, in essence, neither investigated with clarity nor explained in detail. This obviously complicates the work of her interpreters, but it at least has the advantage of putting a somewhat unusual theme at our disposal.

Problematic or not, but promising regardless, natality is perhaps the most original category of thought that Arendt gave to the twentieth century. In Arendt's reflections, birth, rather than being a biological phenomenon (incorporating, for example, the processes of conception, pregnancy, and childbirth), is essentially a scenario, a given of human experience—a theme for the imaginary in much the same way as death has been a theme for philosophy. It should not be forgotten that, for the author of *The Human Condition*, the intention was an explicit and direct challenge: "Natality, and not mortality, may be the central category of political, as distinguished from metaphysical, thought."[23] The figures of the mortal and the dying, so dear to the metaphysical tradition, programmatically give way to the figures of the natal and the nascent. For this reason, Arendt can push her argument and affirm that the miracle of natality, to which her "glad tidings" alludes, concerns "a characteristic of human existence which Greek antiquity ignored altogether."[24] The Greeks, obviously, did not ignore the fact that man is born; as distinct from the Christian tradition, however, they did not produce an imaginary—one could even say, a vast iconological repertoire and an immense literature—on natality. For her part, it should be said, Arendt's sensitivity to this iconological and literary tradition is conspicuously lacking.

Whereas the Christian imaginary of nativity is dominated by the mother-child pair, Arendt's attention when she cites the "glad tidings" remains concentrated exclusively on the newborn. In general, the mother remains unnamed within Arendt's writings, and even more so on this occasion. It is as if the "glad tidings" did not belong to a popular story that has filled the world's churches and galleries with images of the Virgin with the Child. For Arendt, the newborn is the undisputed star of the theater of birth: he steals the scene on the stage where life begins. Even this, however, is a scene of appearance, and as such the newborn is not alone: there are necessarily *others* before whom the child appears. In the Arendtian lexicon, it is worth recalling, appearance is not a generic name but a technical term with an insistently and precisely defined meaning. According to Arendt, one always appears to others. Even if only in the role of "spectators," these others are necessary to the very meaning of appearance insofar as it coincides with being in the world and of the world, or simply with living understood as "being among others" (the Latin concept of *inter homines esse*).[25] Stated differently, in Arendtian terms, the scene of appearance is structurally relational: in it, the *others* are not optional figures but human beings who are materially present, indispensable spectators. Birth, a crucial stage of appearance, obviously does not escape this rule: if the newborn is able to reveal itself as unique and as a beginner, it is because it appears as such to those around it. For this reason, it is at the very least a bit curious that, even though it is plausible that the mother should number among these others, she nevertheless receives no mentions in any of the various passages where Arendt discusses natality and emphasizes its exemplariness. Arendt's reticence on the physical act of giving birth, which keeps her discourse from lapsing into biological digressions, seems to find its counterweight in the absence of the maternal figure, which perhaps also keeps it from lapsing into edifying or sentimental digressions. Even the most distracted interpreter easily will see that the Arendtian newborn, which is completely defined by the function of being a beginning, does not inspire any tenderness. Her representation of natality is, to say the least, quite abstract and cold; lacking in credibility, it is almost an homage to the old philosophical vice of sacrificing the real world's complexity to the purity of the concept. This is probably connected to the way that Arendt calls upon the analogy between first and second birth, which she narrates in numerical order but actually constructs backward. But in fact, despite this logical enumeration, the main scene—which is also central for the entire parable of her political thought—remains the one she designates as the second birth, which is to say, the theater of action. Symptomatically, only this political theater justifies a representation of appearance that, because it is reciprocal and occurs horizontally, can afford to classify those who are present under the generic category of *others*. As Arendt does not tire of repeating, "others," in the human plurality actively called to reveal itself through action, here refers to everyone in their incarnated uniqueness, actor and spectator together on a shared, hence public, space. Because political space does not exist per se but is produced through action, because it is the theatrical *result* of an ontological horizon constituted by interrelations,[26] the space of politics "is the space of appearance in the widest sense of the word, namely, the space where I appear to others as others appear to me, where men exist not merely like other living or inanimate things but make their appearance explicitly."[27] Reciprocity and interdependence are the essential elements of the interactive context she calls politics—the authentic *primum logicum* of the whole Arendtian construction. It is easy to see that these are precisely the elements that are missing from the first and inaugural theater of appearance, in which the newborn is the protagonist. The newborn's situation is obviously not based on mutual appearance and reciprocal revelation. Instead, even though Arendt leaves it aside, the newborn is in a situation of univocal exposure and originary dependence. As in the case of action, relationality is constitutive and structural for the revelation of the human as unique and beginning, but it is of a completely different type. The relations between the characters on the stage—the baby and the *others*, as Arendt would say—do not imply any equality or symmetry. More than the others, understood as mere "spectators," it is the mother who earns herself a prominent role in the inaugural scene. If one eliminates her figure, the scene ends up losing its specific traits, which is to say, the very traits that make the first appearance an originary dependence rather than a theater of interdependence and mutual appearance. It is significant, after all, that such an attentive Arendt interpreter as Peg Birmingham, after having emphasized that "the event of natality is a self-originating origin in so far as it cannot point to something more primordial, something pre-original that would account for its emergency," and after pointing out that "there is no constituting potentiality 'behind the appearance,'" should then affirm that "the originary event proceeds from nothingness."[28] It is perhaps even more significant that, in her political writings, Arendt exalts the category of natality without touching on the theme of infancy. Called upon to incarnate the miracle of the beginning, the Arendtian newborn seems to be entirely consumed in the instant of this exemplary task, thus running the risk of remaining forever a newborn without ever becoming a child or an infant. Within Arendt's theoretical strategy, the newborn does at first appear nascent, but then, stuck in its very paradigmaticity, it does not progress any further—it stops, as it were, being born. This, precisely, is why the mother does not appear on the Arendtian scene. If the newborn's emblematic function is consumed entirely in the act of its appearance, then the maternal figure becomes superfluous. "A child has been born unto us," recite the glad tidings according to Arendt's imprecise citation. The thinker from Hannover, so intent upon defining the characteristics of action, certainly does appreciate the exemplarity of the announcement. But because she isolates it from the Christian imaginary of nativity, she ends up turning it into an abstract formula that is called upon only to illustrate the concept of beginning.

In *The Human Condition*, the terms *birth* and *beginning* are used recurrently and almost interchangeably, but it is symptomatically the latter that defines the former's hermeneutical productivity. Witness, among other things, the way that Arendt's text uses Augustine's aforementioned comment on the Creation story. To explain the fact that men are *initium*, which is to say "newcomers and beginners by virtue of birth," Arendt refers yet again to the words of the philosopher of Hippo: "[Initium] ergo ut esset, creatus est homo, ante quem nullus fuit [That there be a beginning, man was created before whom there was nobody]." Then, glossing this comment, she adds: "This beginning is not the same as the beginning of the world; it is not the beginning of something but of somebody, who is a beginner himself."[29] Arendt's interpretation of Augustine's reading of Genesis hence stresses the correspondence, from the very beginning, between beginning and uniqueness. More precisely, her gloss of Augustine highlights the special status reserved for man in the act of the creation. God does not create him by species, as he does with animals, but in the singular— as a being who, even in his prototype, is unique from the start. The "someone" Arendt mentions, given the context, is therefore evidently Adam. As Arendt of course knows, the truth is that God also creates Eve, but according to her interpretation of this second version of the narrative of Genesis, the passage in question alludes not to the phenomenon of beginning but to the human condition of plurality. "Male and female He created *them*," Arendt quotes from Genesis.[30] She then elaborates: "if we understand that this story of man's creation is distinguished in principle from the one according to which God originally created Man (*adam*),"[31] then we'll notice that the text conveys in an elementary form the human condition of plurality and hence too of action. If the beginning starts not with one but with two who differ from one another, then already at the origin we have a plural reality, which avoids the sense in which "the multitude of human beings becomes the result of multiplication."[32] What is more, and quite symptomatically, the category of plurality reenters the imaginary of the biblical story more easily than does the category of natality. In the creation story, in fact, there is a beginning that resoundingly evokes the origin, but it is not a birth. Adam, like Eve, is created, not procreated. And, it is worth noting, both are created as adults. To the extent that there are here really excellent reasons to eliminate birth and the maternal figure, the scene is therefore perfectly Arendtian. Augustine's words allow Arendt to speak of a concept of birth that is freed even from the embarrassing figure of the newborn—a figure that, for Arendt, is essentially intractable, since it alludes to an unbalanced and unequal relationship that does not fit with her definition of politics as an interaction on a horizontally shared plane.

Even though Arendt doesn't invest the biblical theme of creation with religious or transcendent meanings, it is nevertheless a precious resource for her as she illustrates her concept of beginning. It is also a more or less intentional technique that allows her to uncouple the category of birth from its biological implications and from interference from the imaginary of maternity. In this regard, she can count on illustrious precedents. Whereas the category of birth, the true original point of Arendt's speculation, is indeed almost entirely absent from the metaphysical tradition, the narration of the creation is indeed a habitual reference for philosophy as well as for the history of political thought, from Augustine's *City of God* to the political treatises of early modernity. A perfect example is Locke's *Second Treatise on Civil Government*, where, in order to support his theory of the contract, he appeals to the authority of the sacred book to emphasize how "Adam was created a perfect man, his body and mind in full possession of their strength and reason."[33] Compared to Adam's perfection, which here is the normative paradigm of the "free and intelligent agent," the newborn's condition of dependence is an imperfect state, a long stage of minority that, according to Locke, the male child will have to overcome by becoming a free and independent adult, a full citizen. Not only does this discourse confirm well-known sexist hallmarks of the patriarchal tradition; it also bears the traces of the individualist ontology typical of the political model of modernity, only here in its proto-liberal version. As Kant will not fail to reiterate, the axis around which the subject of the individualistic doctrine revolves is, above all, autonomy. Constructed as self-sufficient and self-referential, radically autonomous, self-enclosed, vertical and straight, the modern individual on principle cannot stand bonds, debts, and dependencies. As Charles Taylor might say, the protagonist of this new theater of subjectivity is a "disengaged self."[34] One can thus understand why infancy, as a state of total dependence, cannot but be seen as an "imperfect state" of the individual who is called upon to reflect Adam's perfection. One also can understand why, in these terms, infancy would be seen as an ontologically annoying and meaningless stage—not unlike birth, a natural event that is also seen as uninteresting.

By removing birth from its irrelevant margin and by placing it at the very center of her political thought, Arendt certainly does contest philosophy's traditional indifference to the event of birth, and does so in a manner at once peremptory and disruptive. But her attempt to project the concept of birth against the background of Adam's creation does not strengthen her disruptive argument. Free though it may be from any hint of individualism, this move actually ends up weakening the novelty of Arendt's political thought and limiting its hermeneutical potential. Her reasoning works only if the scene of birth is used to represent the concept of beginning, which comes at the expense of a phenomenology of natality that would offer the chance to insist on something different: not only and not so much an anti-individualistic rational ontology, but above all a relationality marked by deep asymmetry and by originary dependency. Put bluntly: Adam and the newborn, as Locke noticed, have very little in common. Far from it, in fact: Adam, like Eve, is the only human being never to have been born. Before Eve was created, as one of the versions of the Genesis says, Adam was alone, without any company or relation with his fellow man. Or, as Arendt might have put it: he lacked an other before whom he could appear.

Married twice but childless, perhaps Arendt, like Kant, lacks love for mothers, nannies, and children. Perhaps for this reason she avoids grappling with the stereotype of maternity, even though stereotypes are not always a mere burden for the work of lucid thought. Some, such as those connected to the figure of the mother, even retain great critical potentiality. The experiment of subjecting Arendt's positions to this critical test, in any case, has yielded interesting results. What indeed might we make of Arendt's main thesis—that of a correspondence between the first and second births, between the inaugural theater of birth and the political theater of action—if we introduce a mother into the scene? What might happen to the horizontal relation of reciprocity, which defines politics as the scene of appearance, if it is the unbalanced relationship between the newborn and the mother that serves as a premise for securing the ontological root for action? In the case of Arendt, symptomatically enough, the insertion of the figure of the mother into the scene would fracture its fundamental logical structure. It would disturb the configuration of that scene, showing how it rests on analogies that are more suggestive than probable—analogies that hold only if the newborn is construed methodologically as an orphan and limits itself to playing the beginner's part. There is no life in this theater, neither *zoē* nor *bíos*. Nor is there true relation: just like Adam before a companion was placed at his side, the Arendtian newborn evokes an inhuman loneliness.

12

Schemata for
a Postural Ethics

She had the plump, settled air of a matron
and an inclination to mother and oversee
her husband and brothers as well as her
own children.

Susan Hill, *The Woman in Black*

THE SCENE OF NATALITY, which the iconology of Christian Nativity has culturally appropriated and hyper-represented, rarely passes
through the gateway of official philosophical reflection. When it
does, it is mostly due to feminist reflection on the problem of care,
and hence is generally situated in the field of ethics. In this sense, by
making birth into the central category of ontology and an essential
theme in politics, Arendt opens up a new and as yet unexplored territory of inquiry. For those who want to attempt an exploration of
this issue, however, there remain many obstacles in the way that make
it a very difficult undertaking: from the aforementioned tendency to
censor the stereotype of maternity, an issue which has many different sides in feminist thought, to the all-encompassing biopolitical
paradigm, which aims at limiting birth to the domain of mere procreation. There are also invariably those under the influence of edifying religious ideas or theological questions that inevitably complicate
the matter. And lastly, there is the tendency, especially pronounced

in the wake of Foucault's teachings, to read every relationship, if not also the very concept of relationship itself, in terms of power (and, conversely, to conceive power in relational terms). Even though reading birth in terms of power certainly does account for the mother's complete domination over the infant (a relation that Hobbes's evil genius did not hesitate to identify with the power of destruction),[1] the application of this framework to the imaginary of natality is, in essence, completely misleading: not only does it produce an aberrant portrait of maternity, but above all it risks removing from this imaginary important critical resources for ontology, as well as for ethics and politics. These resources are, in fact, considerable: the imaginary of maternity permits a shift of attention from a subject modeled on the idea of autonomy to a subjectivity structurally characterized by dependence and exposure, from the assertions of a self-consistent and partitioned subjectivity to a subjectivity that is open and relational. In this way, the free and rational subject's supposed integrity, free from all constraint, allows space for an originary and structural vulnerability, which is emphasized precisely in the fateful moment of beginning, when the new creature appears to the world and surrenders to another (who is, normally and in ordinary experience, the mother). In this framework, in other words, birth holds vulnerability and relationality together in an inseparable ontological bond.

Not unlike the very traditional philosophical canon she proposes to oppose in the name of the category of natality, Arendt ends up canceling precisely the reality of this extraordinary experience. Arendt's treatment of birth as "beginning" avoids confronting the given, necessarily asymmetrical, relationship between mother and child—which not only stands in contrast to the equal and horizontal relationality of action, but also insists on a relation in which the newborn's surrender to the mother is irremediable and total. Indeed, as a collective imaginary (which should be dispassionately interrogated, rather than dismissed) attests: the mother herself is at issue—not whoever might take her place or occupy the maternal position. This is also confirmed by a vast critical literature, often psychoanalytical, that never tires of denouncing the various pathologies of the maternal—to the point of including the risk, as Kristeva puts it, that the mother would close herself off "in the omnipotence of an androgynous mother . . . who imagines herself to be fulfilled for the first time through the power that she exerts over her weak child—a child who will no doubt enable her to finally become 'actualized.'"[2] In effect, compared to the cold but harmless speculative role of the Arendtian child, who is born unto us in order to signify the beginning, the condition of the infant who is completely surrendered to the mother's inclination raises a number of questions, and not just in the field of psychoanalysis. Hardly the least of these questions, as Angela Putino observes, is how to strengthen the biopolitical reading of the labor of female caregiving, thus confirming that "the constitutive point of departure of a living being is absolute indigence."[3]

Regarding women's propensity for caregiving, no longer can we postpone inquiry into the famous paradigm of the "ethics of care," which was inaugurated by Carol Gilligan's *In a Different Voice* (1982) and which has largely imposed itself on the scene of contemporary reflection, going well beyond any disciplinary fence.[4] Elaborating her thesis on the basis of empirical research, as Elena Pulcini notes, Gilligan ascribes two different ethical stances to the two genders, "attributing to men the morality inherent to rights and justice, based on abstract and formal principles of equality, and attributing to women an ethics of care and responsibility, based on concrete and contingent criteria of interdependence and relationality."[5] Without underestimating the importance of Gilligan's thesis, it is nevertheless worth pointing out that her position is hardly new. The development of the theme of a contrast between altruism (typical of the maternal and sensitive to concrete relations) and the rational "atomized individual" (typical of modern political doctrine on the subject's autonomy), has been present in feminist thought since its beginning with Mary Wollstonecraft, often resulting in theories that attempt reconciliation between these two positions. The criticism of this binary view—focused on highlighting the qualities of the feminine—is likewise not new within feminism or, above all, within the stream of emancipatory thought that is focused on equality between man and woman with no compromises or distinctions. In the current debate, the accusation that is frequently made specifically against the paradigm of the ethics of care, not only from emancipatory feminism but also from that of a poststructuralist inspiration, is that this model ends up consolidating the patriarchal binary opposition between genders, thereby confirming the self-sacrificing and self-effacing role attributed to women. The stereotype of maternity—some scholars argue—ends up receiving unearned and supplementary credibility, even when, through the lenses of the ethic of care, it is removed from the marginality of the domestic sphere and acquires a potentially universal ethical dignity. Such, at least, is the accusation. Despite the changing epochs and conceptual styles internal to the development of feminist polemic, the argument thus somehow always remains the same: whenever the exercise of thinking human relationality in terms of vulnerability and dependence involves the maternal figure, one invariably finds oneself accused of reinforcing a patriarchal image of woman, forcing one in turn to renounce the operation. This criticism applies in all fields, including the current jagged archipelago of studies that, elaborating on Gilligan's lesson and extending it to the ambit of the political,[6] strive once again to render the relational paradigm of care complementary with the paradigm of individualistic autonomy, in an attempt to think a subjectivity that would deactivate the trap of gender, and within which the two paradigms, instead of being opposed, could temper one another. Today as in the past, in other words, the pattern of complementarity and reconciliation prevails. In a highly valued book, Virginia Held notes, for example, that "political institutions that have the task of governing activities in which the value of care is more obviously relevant may also be greatly improved by considering their design from the perspective of mother/child relations rather than only from the perspective of the liberal rational contractor."[7] In another noteworthy work, Eva Feder Kittay, although severely criticizing the Kantian concept of autonomy, nevertheless insists on "a more adequate representation of persons, one capable of acknowledging dependency as an obligatory limitation to self-governance."[8] Very indicative within this line of thinking is a minor work by Alasdair MacIntyre, in which he acknowledges his indebtedness to Held and Kittey and, reassessing the virtue of care, inquires into the problems of vulnerability and disability. The eloquent title of this volume is *Dependent Rational Animals*;[9] it calls on the idea, shared nowadays by many scholars, that infancy, old age, disease, disability, and other conditions of vulnerability suspend or undermine the individual's full autonomy. Even when the individual's self-sufficiency is methodologically put in question, in other words, it nevertheless continues to operate as a standard for a general definition of the human. For MacIntyre, in fact, infancy as the emblematic situation of vulnerability and dependence continues to be inscribed within a necessary trajectory of growth, one that takes the child from dependence to an equally emblematic condition of being "one independent practical reasoner" who relates to "other independent practical reasoners as well as to those who in turn at some later stage become dependent on her or him."[10] In the conviction that the exercise of "independent practical reason" is an "essential ingredient" of childhood development,[11] MacIntyre's thesis essentially attempts to reconcile the virtues of an independent rational agent with the virtues of recognized dependence. Thus, in MacIntyre's conceptualization, the condition of dependence, of vulnerability, doesn't function as the essential archetype of the human, as its constitutive and untranscendable horizon, but as a state of weakness that debilitates a being that is otherwise thought as archetypically autonomous and independent. His work does not then radically contest the paradigm of the liberal individual; he merely reforms and corrects it by interjecting the condition of dependence as a recurrent but temporary possibility for everyone, such that, apart from especially unfortunate cases (involving, for example, severe disability), all can claim it as a universal condition that is equivalent and complementary to the classic principle of autonomy. The framework, moreover, aims to apply to everyone, irrespective of the sex, not only of the creature who is in the contingent state of dependency, but also—on an ethical basis of perfect reciprocity—of the one who takes care, or should take care of, that creature. Stated in a brief formula: interdependence and reciprocity become fundamental categories that apply to everyone, thus universalizing the circumstances

of dependency and vulnerability, which, combined with the unques-
tioned universality of the principle of autonomy, are integrated into
a new model that at last gets rid of the gender stereotypes associated
with both sexes. After all, was not everyone at some point an infant?
And what prevents men as well as women from taking care of infants
and of vulnerable creatures in general?

About twenty years after the publication of Arendt's *Human Condition*, her old friend Hans Jonas wrote a book that aimed at designing
a global ethics for a technological world. In *The Imperative of Responsibility*, Jonas states that "with every newborn child humanity begins
anew, and in that sense also the responsibility for the continuation is
involved."[12] Especially when Jonas notes the newborn's "wholly contingent uniqueness" for which the child's parents are now responsible,[13] his reference to the newborn's uniqueness and unpredictability
recalls Arendt's reflections on natality. Much less Arendtian, however,
is Jonas's central thesis, which sees the paradigm of responsibility in
the newborn, whose "mere breathing uncontradictably addresses an
ought to the world around, namely, to take care of him."[14] For Jonas,
this originary paradigm "is not only in terms of self-evidence and
content the archetype of all responsibility, but also its initial germ in
the generic human condition" (or, more precisely, its germinal roots:
Keime).[15] There is no doubt a notable distance, almost a contrast, between the mode in which Arendt treats natality and Jonas's proposal,
which calls on the newborn in order to ground responsibility in the
category of "duty," and even to postulate an obligatory altruism toward
humanity and the whole planet. Jonas's newborn, as the archetype of
an extreme vulnerability and as an imperative demand for care, thus
becomes not only a paradigm for the vulnerability of all humanity,
but also an appeal to preserve humanity itself, as part of an environ-
ment and a living world that are threatened in their totality. Paying a
symptomatic homage to the metaphysical tradition, Jonas roots his
theoretical work in the philosophical rule that insists upon the absolute priority of Being over Nothingness. Aside from this and other
no less alarming conceptual drifts, which greatly complicate the picture and threaten to make it abstract, Jonas's discourse on the new-

born nevertheless contains an element of concreteness that, especially when compared to Arendt, we would do well to appreciate. When Jonas describes the scene of birth, in which the human announces itself as dependent and vulnerable, he does not focus on the newborn alone. To the contrary, Jonas includes the *other* who is called upon to respond to the newborn's presence—who is, presumably, the mother, even if it is true that Jonas speaks more generally of "parents."

To fully appreciate the completeness of Jonas's conceptualization, it remains important to see whether (and, if so, to what extent) the mother (or anyone else who may fulfill this role) also partakes in the same state of vulnerability that is so openly exhibited by the newborn; or whether the mother does not, in fact, partake in this vulnerability at all—whether, in other words, she is strangely exempted, removed, and dispensed with. If the former, we would witness a scene involving a responsible person who partakes of the state of vulnerability common to all humans, yet who manifests that vulnerability from a different angle—or better, with a different posture, indeed with a different leaning [*piegatura*]. If the latter, on the other hand, we would find a postural archetype of responsibility that conforms to the vertical line on the Cartesian plane of duty (which is certainly more in line with Jonas's thought). But this, of course, would run counter to any credible image of natality and maternity.

Even Jonas's analysis thus helps us only up to a certain point; although interesting, his scene of the newborn remains abstract and essentially vertical. If there's a geometry of responsibility in Jonas, it is one that yet again avoids organizing itself along an inclined line: maternal inclination—understood as a posture that is relational, originary, and asymmetrical, capable of evoking a common vulnerability—is not in the picture. In order to reorganize the picture's coordinates, in fact, we would need a different optics, a radical change of perspective. It obviously would be insufficient simply to thematize natality and maternity in their own terms, as if they somehow contained an exclusive sense or essentially embodied some possible or ideal relation. Even less to the point would be to infantilize the human, to maternalize ethics, or to proceed along the lines mapped out by so-

called "maternal thinking."[16] Instead, in light of the verticality that
dominates the history of ontology, the task is to change our register
or reposition our gaze, trying to imagine ontology as a geometry of
variable postures inside of which inclination may assume a "modular"
role. When our questioning calls upon a relational rather than individualistic model, and hence too on an altruistic rather than selfish
subject, inclination can become the module that composes the picture's design—its leitmotif or prevailing posture. This, needless to say,
contrasts quite strikingly with the naturalistic viewpoint that takes for
granted the notion that erect posture is somehow special, and that
accepts the situatedness of the species *Homo* in a vertically oriented
visual field as an objective, incontrovertible, and obvious fact. Put
in anthropological terms, the vertical posture, which coincides with
the line of gravity, produces an intuition of space that turns the body
into the standard of "absolute qualities" (such as above, below, fast,
slow, etc.).[17] The simple fact that humans walk upright, using an erect
posture, already contains an implicit geometry, supposedly immediate and natural, that is organized according to dimensions, lines,
locations, and topologies which are, in turn, defined with reference
to the absolute orientation of corporeal verticality. This self-evidence
is inescapable, and it obviously would be futile and absurd to avoid
this matter of fact together with the formidable symbolic prolifera-
tion that confirms its power. Far less absurd, however, and in fact
even theoretically promising, is the effort to reinterrogate the truth
of the zoological structure in the name of the relational model, which
in many respects maternal inclination illustrates and emphasizes. On
the speculative plane, the challenge is not to ignore or negate the self-
evidence of the vertical model, but to critique its limits, its pretenses,
and its uncritical adoption in the fields of ontology, ethics, and politics. Besides questioning whether, how, to what extent—and at what
cost!—the geometry intrinsic to *Homo erectus* adapts itself to all the
realms of meaning in which the human manifests its condition, it is in
fact philosophically even more urgent to ask what consequences this
geometry produces for our discourses on subjects, human relations,
and community.

From this perspective, the verticalizing systems of Plato, Hobbes, Locke, Kant, Canetti, but also Augustine, Anselm, Thomas, and other milestones of western philosophy are paradigmatic. Just as paradigmatic is the insistence, above all during modernity, on an autarchic and egoistic model, which recently has faced increasing opposition from the relational and altruistic model. Distilled from stereotypical pictures that are centuries old, restyled as a geometry that is perhaps not immediately naturalistic but rather very realistic, maternal inclination helps us to explore exactly this latter model. The mother bent over her child: precisely this gesture allows inclination to be deployed strategically as a good point of departure for rethinking the ontology of the vulnerable, together with its constitutive relationality, in terms of a postural geometry that, far from limiting itself to the axis of uprightness, arranges the human along multiple coexisting lines, which may be contingent and intermittent, and at times even random. Maternal inclination, by virtue of its connection to the scenario of natality, may then become a new fundamental schematism—the gestural mark of a new postural geometry, a new mode for evaluating the terrain of the encounter. This does not mean, of course, that all asymmetrical relations that pertain to this new geometry repeat the radical imbalance between mother and child. Nor does it even mean that all postural variants are simple reproductions of the inclined position, varying only in the degree of their fidelity. It does mean, however, that within this new relational ontology of the vulnerable, understood geometrically, the centrality of the vertical posture, which is so dear to the sovereign individual and to its dreams of autonomy, now appears much more improbable. Understood in terms of relational ontology, all schemata based on verticality and symmetry are, in essence, an anomaly. It would be a pathetic blunder to theorize a subject that "shores itself up, seeks to reconstitute its imagined wholeness, but only at the price of denying its own vulnerability, its dependency, its exposure."[18]

Perhaps the glad tidings to which Arendt wished to direct our attention, besides coaxing us to reflect on birth, should be understood as a warning against mistakes and anomalies of this sort. *A child has been born unto us*: if the scene of the beginning decides the character of a human ontology that definitively subtracts itself from the subject's metaphysical protocols, then the corresponding geometric imaginary will not include any solitary verticalization. Adam, who was created as "a perfect man," probably did assume an erect posture right away. Those born from women, by contrast, evoke a kind of subjectivity already caught up in folds, dependencies, exposures, dramas, knots, and bonds. However grounded in a naturalistic intuition of space it may seem to be, the individual who is vertically encapsulated in its autarchic pretense—in its freedom, autonomy, and independence—has no actual correspondence to real life. A subject of this sort is a fictitious entity, a mirage—an invention of a philosophical mind that is in tune with modern politics, and that reinstalls the verticality of paternal authority in the horizontal plane of fraternal equality.

In a famous chapter of *Totem and Taboo*, Freud narrates originary patricide as the violent act that founds civilization: the sons kill and eat the father in order to constitute a society comprised of brothers. A few years later, Hans Kelsen wrote a more distinctly political version of the story, maintaining that "so far as the archetype of all authority is the father, since that is the original experience of authority, democracy—in Idea, that is—is a fatherless society. It seeks so far as possible, to be a leaderless association of equals."[19] Put simply: the model of modern democracy, which is based on an individualistic ontology, is marked by relations that are horizontal, not on relations that are vertical, based on hierarchies of higher and lower.[20] This is confirmed by the revolutionary motto of modern politics: *liberté, egalité, fraternité*. In the new era, however—as Hobbes noted long before the French Revolution—the father's verticality does not disappear, but reappears in different forms (in the emblem printed on the frontispiece of the *Leviathan*, for instance, which warns of a structural, modular verticality that will impose its straightening effect upon the horizontal and democratic matter of which the modern state consists). In any case, it is instructive that, according to various political revisitations of Freud's narrative, the dimension of verticality is embodied in the figure of the father, while the dimension of horizontality is embodied in the figure of the brothers: not only is the background of this discourse undeniably phallocentric, but the very assumption of male figures as geometrical archetypes of political systems, along with their role in structuring kinship, encourages us to imagine an alternative political order organized instead on feminine postural archetypes. Critics, including but not only feminists, have often and even too emphatically spoken of matriarchal societies and the mythical time of the Mothers. Maternal inclination could work as a module for a different, more disruptive, and revolutionary geometry whose aim is to rethink the very core of community.

Coda

Adieu to Lévinas

IN THE SPEECH HE DELIVERED at Emmanuel Lévinas's funeral to
bid adieu, Jacques Derrida claimed that it was from Lévinas that he
first learned the sense of the word *uprightness* and began "to understand it otherwise."[1] In Lévinas's works, the term *rectitude* (*droiture*)
does not have a generic sense; it appears mainly in reference to the
face-to-face encounter with the other, that is to say, an ethical context in which the "extreme rectitude of the face of the neighbor," as
well as the uprightness of "an exposure unto death,"[2] interpellates me
personally and calls me to respond. Bound up as it is with the themes
of responsibility and death—but also of transcendence, the infinite,
and Lévinas's anomalous sense of ethics—the question is complex; to
truly bid it 'adieu,' it must be examined patiently. At the outset, however, it is useful to touch on the curious discrepancy between what
Benjamin wrote in his youthful fragment on inclination and the fundamental role that Lévinas instead reserves for rectitude. Although
the two authors are distant and uncomparable, the common Jewish
matrix of which they are very different expressions nevertheless seems
to authorize this sort of comparison. In terms of geometric imaginary,
their positions demonstrate a contrast: while Benjamin suggests that
a rethinking of the concept of inclination could change our idea of
the moral, Lévinas evokes the concept of rectitude to redefine eth-

ics through a radical transformation. If it is true, as Arendt reminds us, that the centrality of the self conceals an important problem for philosophy in general, and for ethics in particular, then the work of Lévinas indeed alters the picture radically. His ethics dethrones the self and instead recenters itself upon the other. He substitutes structural egotism with "a total altruism."[3]

One of the main threads running throughout the work of Lévinas may be defined synthetically as a critique of egology. Lévinas denounces the presence, above all in modern philosophy, of a system founded on the self's speculative totalitarianism—which is to say, of a subject conceived as free, autopoietic, and solipsistic. In contrast, possibly alluding to Hegel, Lévinas observes that "the self itself has not issued from its own initiative, as it claims in the plays and figures of consciousness on the way to the unity of an Idea."[4] Far from occupying a special place, the Hegelian system is just a variant internal to the tradition of European philosophy, which was inaugurated by the Greek *logos* and remains indebted to Parmenides' thought, and which Lévinas contests through an original recuperation of Jewish wisdom. In the tradition that is here placed under examination in its entirety, the celebrated Cartesian Cogito constitutes an exemplary case: both as a model of an autarchic and self-sufficient subject that generates itself through thought, and as a model of thinking—of representing, recognizing, and knowing—that is rooted in "comprehension," which is to say that, literally, "seizing" or "taking hold" it grasps the other in order to integrate it within the self, assimilating the other in the totality of the system. "And the first-person present verb of the *cogito*," writes Lévinas, "includes the thinkable in its totality and thus constitutes the autonomy of knowledge, which is self-supporting and fathers itself in the systematic unity to which the consciousness of an 'I' lends itself. From whence the integration into the system . . . of all that can seem *other* in succession."[5] In the horizon of philosophy as egology, the other is not there—or, at least, not there in the way that Lévinas understands it, which is to say, as the radically Other who is absolutely external to the I, and who is given prior to any comprehension, knowledge, or even thematization, in the event of the face-to-face encounter. It is precisely this encounter—which traumatically eradicates subjectivity from "egoism or egotism and, in any case, 'egology,'"[6] and which establishes Lévinasian ethics as relational and *for the other*— that Lévinas counterposes to the totalizing ontology of the *for oneself.*

In Lévinas's work, the critique of egology is inscribed in a general critique of philosophy as ontology. Egology itself has been a genuine expression, ever since the movement of Socratic truth, which produces itself internally to the subject. "Philosophy is an egology,"[7] Lévinas declares, and it is such well before modernity and the Cartesian Cogito. Born with Parmenides and unable to free itself from the Greek spirit that still dominates it, the philosophical tradition from the very beginning has had the bad habit of posing the unity of being as its principle and of using the logic of the Same as its all-inclusive movement. Being and thinking are the same and are all—*en kai pan*, as Parmenides notoriously puts it.[8] For Lévinas, "knowledge of being in general, or fundamental ontology,"[9] as a characteristic trait of philosophical knowledge from the Presocratics to Heidegger in its various articulations, concerns precisely this coincidence between being and thinking, which configures itself as a closed totality, as an omnipotent knowledge that not only does not allow for the other, but also seems to reabsorb any discourse about the Other in the language of the Same. In this sense, even the simple task of talking about an alterity that is irreducible to the system is, in itself, a radical challenge to the "formal immanentism" of the western *logos*.[10] This explains why Lévinas, taking on this challenge, strives to develop a "non-ontological language," and addresses the paradox to having to use the same language he intends to go beyond.[11] *Totality and Infinity* has the subtitle *An Essay on Exteriority*. For the self-reflective and all-encompassing subject, in fact, nothing is exterior. The Cogito constitutes the paradigm of "a total adequation of the thinker with what is thought, in the very precise sense of a mastery exercised by the thinker upon what is thought, in which the object's resistance as an exterior being vanishes."[12] The systematic unity of consciousness, inasmuch as it is a totality, is allergic to exteriority. The alterity of the Other, according to Lévinas, expresses its structural exteriority precisely vis-à-vis the tyranny of the I as a closed totality, all-comprehending and self-sufficient. The Other—and it is not by chance that Lévinas often marks it with a capital letter—is exactly what the congenital interiority of the I cannot "com-prehend" or conceptualize. In this sense, it is beyond the grasp of egology and its system of representation and inclusion. The Other is therefore the transcendent—indeed, it is absolute transcendence compared to the system's principle, its *arché*, and it is therefore "an-archic." As his interpreters know, it is not easy to orient oneself in Lévinas's writing without stumbling over enigmatic terms such as this—which, moreover, are inserted into an altogether peculiar vocabulary and an often exhausting phrasing, which occasionally require word-by-word explanation. For the sake of brevity, and at the risk of betraying its complex texture, the theme of exteriority may then be appropriate to provide the beginning of an initial and convenient schematization. Because the language of philosophy—its network of nouns, concepts, and meanings—"converts all *Other* into *Same*" before the pursuit even begins,[13] Lévinas's main problem is precisely a problem of language: because "the same and the other can not enter into a cognition that would encompass them,"[14] the problem is essentially to find the words to vocalize, express, and describe an order of sense that, despite being contained in the cage of the system's language, is nonetheless able to exceed and escape that very cage. In its elementary structure, the problem is obviously not altogether new: it could indeed even be said that the whole history of philosophy, if not also philosophy itself, is an uninterrupted meditation on language and its untranscendability. By situating the encounter with the Other in a place that is by definition exterior to the grip of discourse, Lévinas gives this perennial problem a special twist. Formulated in simple terms—and taking into account that Lévinas's entire oeuvre traces the Other, in writing as in speech—this then is the question: how does one speak of the Other's exteriority, of his absolute alterity, without also absorbing the Other into the language of the Same? How does one speak of an ethical movement that prescribes an an-archic orientation of the I toward the Other—a preoriginary opening, a primordial attitude vis-à-vis one's encounter with the Other—through a language produced, dominated, and presided over by "a subject turned in on itself"?[15] In other words, and even more paradoxically, how does one speak of a relation with the Other that, according to Lévinas, is the foundation of language itself, yet is also anterior to and "irreducible to comprehension"?[16] Lévinas's paratactic and quasi-oracular prose is filled with adjectives such as *an-archic, pre-originary, primordial, anterior, primeval,* and so on. Far from being merely stylistic mannerisms, Lévinas's fastidious recourse to these terms marks his attempt to respond to these crucial questions. The same applies to the obsessive recurrence of expressions such as *au-delà* ("on the other side") or *en deçà* ("on this side"). As Lévinas grapples with the paradox of conceptualizing what he himself postulates as non-thematizable and non-conceptualizable, he may commit linguistic abuse but he nevertheless follows a precise strategy. If the system nominates and dominates the concept of the origin, what exceeds the system can only qualify as pre-originary, an-archic. If egology is configured as a totality, what exceeds it can only situate itself *au-delà* or *en deçà.* In terms of space and time, this means *before* and *outside,* but, as Lévinas ceaselessly points out, it also means *above* and *beyond,* or more specifically, *Height.* In fact, Lévinas's "non-ontological language" is full of metaphors related to the order of space, if not quite to the vocabulary of geometry. From this point of view, the noun *uprightness* [*droiture*] is in good company.

Good, yet equivocal. Whereas Lévinas grapples willingly with the category of "time," indeed turning it into one of the most decisive and most interesting themes of his ethical conception, he has a clear and motivated hostility toward the category of "space," and even more toward the achievement of visibility that any spatial conceptualization presupposes. It is the deeply Jewish vein of his thought that causes this attitude. Inaugurated by the Platonic Idea, the register of the visible marks the whole story of western philosophy—which is to say, precisely, ontology, which was born in Greece, and against which Lévinas also, and especially, battles in the name of the invisible God of the Jewish tradition. Curiously, however, Lévinas spares from his critique one of Plato's most celebrated passages, which over time became both a blessing and a curse for an immense critical literature. This is the renowned passage from the *Republic*, where Plato describes the idea of Good, affirming that the Good itself is *epekeina thes ousias*,[17] or in Lévinas's translation, "au-delà de l'essence [beyond essence]." "Plato nowise deduces being from the Good: he posits transcendence as surpassing the totality," Lévinas comments.[18] A principle that dwells in a place that is other and superior, higher than the actual knowledge of the truth itself, the Good exceeds the system and transcends it—or, to put it in the Lévinasian lexicon, it escapes from its com-prehension. That Lévinas should appreciate this excess is not surprising. What is a bit surprising, however, is that he would go so far as to appreciate the comparison between the Good and the sun proposed by Plato, even though his interest unsurprisingly emphasizes the description of a dazzling sun that, blinding the eyes, renders itself invisible. Nonetheless, the Lévinasian recuperation of Plato remains somewhat problematic. On the one hand, the sun of the *Republic* is a luminous star, the very source of the light that allows visible things to be seen, and that gives the sense of sight its capacity to see. The heliotropic metaphor presupposes the analogy between visibility and intelligibility and celebrates the "cold splendor" of Plato's *theoria* of ideas.[19] On the other hand, in the parable of the cave, as Lévinas doesn't fail to note, the eye gradually becomes accustomed to the light until, inevitably, "the sun is not forever removed from the gaze."[20] In that same parable, it should be added, the one who manages to overcome the phase of bedazzlement and finally to look toward the sun is none other than the philosopher, the contemplator of ideas who ultimately rights himself along the vertical axis of truth at whose apex is the Good. The solar metaphor that organizes Platonic discourse, besides reinforcing the correspondence between visible order and intelligible order, refers explicitly to a geometrical imaginary, and, to be precise, to a conception of space dominated by the vertical line. For this reason, moreover, Plato can speak logically of a top and bottom, an upper and a lower, and, not least, of a philosopher who rises up, looks above himself, straightens himself up, and stands still and erect. But because Lévinas resists on principle the category of space, his use of expressions such as *au-delà* or *en deçà*, as well as his insistence on *rectitude* and *height*, appear rather less convincing. Or, at the very least, they appear to be symptoms of a geometry that is latent and speculatively unresolved. His sympathy for Plato is thus a clue that is both important and worrisome. How many interpreters have noticed that even his fundamental thesis on the irreducibility of the Other to the Same is also plainly Platonic? Daring to "break with Parmenides" and to commit the famous parricide,[21] Plato theorizes it in *The Sophist*, where he distinguishes the Other (*to heteron*) from the Same (*tauton*) and, on an epistemological register, gives them equal dignity. Crucially, however, these remain only categories of thought, of speculative "genres," of articulations internal to discourse. Plato's *to heteron* is not the other man.

In the course of the analysis he develops in *Totality and Infinity*, as he does in the rest of his writings, Lévinas claims continuously that the encounter with the Other comes first through the face of the other as another man. The aim of the work is to define the "primacy of the ethical, that is, of the relationship of man to man—signification, teaching, and justice—a primacy of an irreducible structure upon which all the other structures rest."[22] In the "face-to-face" encounter, which establishes the ethical relation, the face of the other is human: whether it is written with the capital letter or not, the other is precisely the other man. As suggested by one of the titles of his books, Lévinas's *Humanism of the Other* is in polemic with the philosophical currents of twentieth-century antihumanism or posthumanism. As Lévinas does not fail to emphasize, even the things of the world and the world itself, inasmuch as they are external to the self, also evoke, as Plato tells us, the category of alterity. If ethics decisively invokes the other as other man, then the phenomenology of alterity expands to include the other in general as object. The egological system introjects and absorbs this alterity, so that every external object disappears in the totalizing logic of the Same. In an interesting section of *Totality and Infinity*, Lévinas decides to excavate this logic from a critical perspective that contrasts with its totalizing structure. The principal purpose of his analysis is to expose the relations between the I and the alterity of things concealed within the system of the Same; at the same time, he wants to illustrate the formation of the I as separation from anonymous and indistinct being. By overturning the structure of the Cartesian Cogito, while also parodying Hegel's description of the itinerary of *The Phenomenology of Spirit* and trying to go further back than Husserl's intentional consciousness, Lévinas begins the inquiry by situating the genesis of the I, not within thought and consciousness, but in sensibility.

The I identified with reason degrades the body into a mere support if not a prison, tending to subjugate corporeal sensibility to the exigencies of rational knowledge, and to see bodily needs as a disturbing residue of animality. Lévinas reevaluates sensibility and overturns precisely this perspective. Sensibility, for him, is not a "stammering thought, condemned to error and illusion," nor is it even "a mere spring board for rational knowledge."[23] It is instead the genuine realm of life "in the sense that we speak of the enjoyment of life": it is the sphere where material needs are satisfied, where we have enjoyment, and where "the egoism of the I pulsates."[24] The other, for this corporeal and pre-reflexive I, is first of all the food it eats or the air it breathes or the land on which it rests, but not because these elements provide nourishment for the preservation of life—the famous *conatus essendi* of the self turned inward toward itself—but precisely as enjoyment of that nourishment. Need nurtures enjoyment, an enjoyment that is "beyond instinct, beneath reason," and which "is accomplished when *I stand* in the world."[25] The phrase "I stand"—yet another mark, hardly accidental, of a latent geometry—should be taken literally. After pointing out that the I of sensibility, immersed in the actuality of its unreflected enjoyment, will have to worry about tomorrow and turn to work, Lévinas clarifies that "labor . . . already requires discourse and consequently the height of the other irreducible to the same, the presence of the Other. There is no natural religion; but already human egoism leaves pure nature *by virtue of the human body raised upwards,* committed in the *direction of height. This is not its empirical illusion but its ontological production and its ineffaceable testimony.* The 'I can' proceeds from this height."[26]

The italics are Lévinas's, and there is no need to emphasize that, in this quotation there are several geometric indices. At a first glance, it still looks like a glorification of the meta-empirical meaning of erect posture, one that is not too different from the sort that Herder proposes. The corporeal and natural I, having already left the state of pure nature that obviously concerns other animals, is upright: it straightens itself from the bottom up. In Lévinas's vision, however, this phenomenon assumes a very complex and peculiar significance. For him, erect posture proves first of all that the human being, insofar as it is corporeal, is structurally predisposed to the relationship between man and man that occurs through the "face-to-face" encounter, which in turn constitutes the fundamental principle of ethics. It is also testimony, in an incontestable way, to an originary strain toward height, more specifically towards that Highness of the divine dimension that, for Lévinas, opens itself through the human face.[27]

And this is, notoriously, one of the finer points of Lévinasian thought and of its various interpretations. The question of the divine, of a God who speaks through the face of the other man—complicated by Lévinas's recourse to capital letters, which is enigmatic and not always transparent—is one of the most discussed problems in the vast critical literature dedicated to his work. Aware of the problem and of possible misinterpretations, Lévinas explained in an interview that, "as I see it, it is not a question of God encountered outside of humans. I have always spoken of the perspective of height that opens itself through the human."[28] Elsewhere, referring to the Judaic tradition that influences his thought, he recalls that Majesty and Highness are traditional characteristics of the biblical God: Psalm 113, Lévinas notes, "sings of 'the elevation above all the nations and the glory above the heavens' of 'our God that is enthroned on high'"; but He "looketh down low upon heaven and upon the earth."[29] At the beginning of *Totality and Infinity*, when he introduces the theme of alterity as exteriority and transcendence, Lévinas clarifies that "it is understood as the alterity of the Other and of the Most-High," as "the very dimension of height."[30] The problematic quality of the quote, significantly, does not escape the notice of Derrida, who, in an essay on *Totality and Infinity*, while considering "the resemblance between man and God," wonders if Lévinas would have agreed with the "infinitely ambiguous sentence from the *Book of Questions* by Edmond Jabès: "All faces are His; this is why HE has no face.'"[31] In fact, it is hard to refrain from the conjecture that, in Lévinas's writing, terms such as the "Most High" and "Highness" refer unequivocally to God, resulting in much difficulty for scholars who engage with and decipher his texts. It is likewise difficult not to notice the geometric imaginary that innervates his writing, so that it is easy to conclude that erect posture, for Lévinas, marks a predisposition toward the Highness of the divine and, at the same time, an alignment along the perpendicular line of His Highness. If this is true, then the Lévinasian framework would be the same as the one illustrated in Barnett Newman's *Adam*: man's erect posture, as well as man's bond with God, can be represented as a straight bar.

In *Humanism of the Other*, Lévinas writes about the fact that ethics discovers "the dimension of elevation."

> Elevation introduces a sense into being. This is already experienced in the human body. It leads human societies to erect altars. It is not because men experience verticality in their bodies that the human is placed under the sign of elevation, it is because being is ordained by elevation that the human body is placed in a space where top and bottom are distinguished and the sky is discovered, the sky that Tolstoy's Prince André described—with not a word about colors—as elevation, pure elevation.[32]

Rather than just being one dimension of space, the height of His Highness orders its verticality, so to speak, producing the configuration to which man's erect posture conforms. With reference to the section of *Totality and Infinity* here under discussion, it should not be forgotten, however, that the I who assumes an erect posture through enjoyment is just a figure that Lévinas examines in order to understand how sensibility relates to alterity. Such is the relationship, but here it remains latent: it marks a dependency that the sensible I mistakes for independence. The "I" in its erect posture, "constituting itself in the happiness of enjoyment," Lévinas writes, "does not institute an absolute subjectivity, independent of the non-I."[33] The non-I (which is to say, alterity in the form of food, water, and everything the I enjoys) marks a condition of dependence that the enjoying I does not sense as such. "Egoist without reference to the Other," the I of enjoyment is "alone without solitude, innocently egoist and alone," feeding on an external reality toward which it remains deaf and indifferent—"without ears, like a hungry stomach."[34] Enjoyment, in which the I becomes erect and quivers, crystallizes the I as an absolute island of egoity, immersed in the indistinct sea of an alterity unknown to the I who enjoys it. More than just a relation with the other self, as Lévinas particularly likes to keep emphasizing, this is a *separation* from the chaotic and indistinct alterity from which the self takes pleasure. It is worth meditating on the recurring plastic figures through which Lévinas describes the genesis of the self. It develops its upright posture through a separation from the impersonal totality of what simply *is there* (*il y a*)—from the anonymous and insensate buzz of indistinct being, from being understood as an *apeiron* that resists identification.[35] "Enjoyment is a withdrawal into oneself, an involution, a vibrant exaltation in which dawns the self. For the I is not the *support* of enjoyment . . . the I is the very contraction of sentiment, the pole of a spiral whose coiling and involution is drawn by enjoyment: the focus of the curve is a part of the curve. It is precisely as a 'coiling,' as a movement toward oneself, that enjoyment comes into play."[36]

The spiral of enjoyment that generates the I, separating it as *unique* being from the totality of impersonal being, develops irresistibly as a centripetal vortex that rises to the top, moving vertically. Upright like Adam, "at the origin there is a being gratified, a citizen of paradise."[37] "In the happiness of enjoyment is enacted the individuation, the auto-personification, the sub-stantialization, and the independence of the self," Lévinas points out. "Enjoyment is the very production of a being that is *born*, that breaks the tranquil eternity of its seminal or uterine existence to enclose itself in a person, who in living from the world lives at home with itself."[38] Here as before, the italics are Lévinas's and signal, at the very least, his embarrassment at the use of the verb *to be born*, that is to say, his discomfort over the scenario the verb inevitably evokes: a childbirth, a mother, a baby. What worries him, and what his italics distance him from, is symptomatically the possibility that the I of enjoyment—this "fulfilled being," immersed in the happiness of nourishment, this creature who depends on the other without knowing it—will be mistaken for a child born from a maternal body, uterine home of quiet and impersonal existence, site of the *il y a*. What if, after all, the I of enjoyment was not born immediately upright? Is it not precisely its congenitally erect posture that is supposed to orient it toward Highness, predisposing it to its encounter with the rectitude of the face? Indeed, in contrast to Adam, the figure of the newborn would seem to be the least suited to incarnate the archetype—the I that is born upright—that Lévinas here discusses. It is also well known, and not just to his feminist interpreters, that the treatment Lévinas reserves for the themes of maternity, Woman, and the feminine is equivocal and structurally ambiguous. As Derrida puts it, one can recognize in Lévinas's texts the mark of a "classical androcentrism," or even an "androcentric hyperbole."[39] We find a striking example in *Totality and Infinity*, in the chapter on the "home," or the "house," that gives shelter to the pre-reflective I and allows it to pass from enjoyment to labor.

The dimension of time, and with it concern for the future, "destroys the security of instantaneous happiness" sought by the I of enjoyment, but also "permits the fragility thus discovered to be overcome" through labor.[40] "And it is the relation with the other," Lévinas adds, "inscribed in the body as its elevation, that makes possible the transformation of enjoyment into consciousness and labor."[41] Such is the next stage of the development of the I, according to Lévinas's reconstruction that overturns the system of the Cogito and mimics the trajectory of Hegel's *Phenomenology of Spirit*, starting with sensibility, with consciousness yet to come. In the sequence of events that rips the I away from "this animal complacency in oneself,"[42] the first step forward is indeed labor, in which "the primordial technique does not put into practice an antecedent 'knowledge,' but has immediately a hold on matter."[43] The overall picture, regarding the congenital verticality of the I, remains completely coherent. For Lévinas, the innate erect posture that predisposes the I toward Highness also predisposes it to labor: "I exist as a body, that is, as erect, an organ that will be able to grasp and consequently place itself, in this world on which I depend, before technically realizable ends."[44] The erect posture frees up the hands for work, anthropologists would say more simply. They would add that the dwelling place is an important part of human evolution. For his part, Lévinas underlines that the I, to situate itself in the world, needs an abode, a shelter away from the world itself, in which to gather itself: "man abides in the world as having come to it from a private domain, from being at home with himself, to which at each moment he can retire."[45] "Labor," Lévinas continues, "is the very *en-ergy* of acquisition. It would be impossible in a being that had no dwelling place."[46] The abode is indeed such a dwelling place, "a retreat home with oneself as in a land of refuge," a reception that refers to a welcome and, more precisely, to a feminine welcome and reception.[47] Since "the interiority of recollection is a solitude in a world already human," the intimacy of domestic space presupposes "an *intimacy with someone*," which is to say Woman, "the other whose presence is discreetly an absence, with which is accomplished the primary hospitable welcome which describes the field of intimacy."[48] For Lévinas, woman is distinct from the alterity of things, and yet she remains the ambiguous incarnation of a faceless human Other. She is, Lévinas writes, the expression of "a delightful lapse in being, and the source of gentleness in itself," a creature who stays reserved "on the ground of the full human personality."[49] More citations would ultimately just make the picture even worse, but even here there is already enough to draw attention to the classic androcentrism that dominates the text. Silent angel of the home, Woman is at the service of an exquisitely virile I that, far from being born of a woman, erects itself through enjoyment.

Lévinas's work, despite the notable shifts that characterize its long itinerary, aims tenaciously at denouncing the intrinsic violence within the subject of the philosophical tradition, built upon the logic of the Same and allergic to the Other. This is a subject conceived in terms of power and enclosed within itself. Lévinas does not hesitate to define it as virile, sovereign, fierce, and heroic—a Ulysses of sorts who, even when he faces the vicissitudes of the roaming adventures that lead him to explore the other (as Hegel teaches us), ends up incorporating his alterity, returning at the finish to the point from which he started, thus moving in a circle within the island of his own system. The odyssey of consciousness in Hegel's *Phenomenology of Spirit* provides an exemplary portrait of this circular movement: even if on less dialectical shores, and in a way that is perhaps more important for modernity, this hypothesis is confirmed by the multiplication of free and rational (or really, ferocious and life-thirsty) selves of which individualistic ontology speaks. The insular I of the individualistic doctrine admits the existence of other selves, insofar as they are replicas of the Same—selves thought as autonomous and self-enclosed, who distribute themselves along a horizontal plane on the basis of relations of reciprocity and symmetry. This doctrine programmatically rejects what for Lévinas is the Other with the capital O—an other, perhaps, on which the I depends and which hence demystifies any pretense of integrity and self-sufficiency. This is why Lévinas can claim that "the resistance of the Other to the Same is the failure of philosophy."[50] This is also why, if we could now strategically abandon all uppercase words, the other who brings the newborn into the world, and welcomes it in its absolute nudity, would mark the failure of the theory of the subject. It is improbable, though, that Lévinas would subscribe to the latter statement, despite the many poignant pages he dedicated to the theme of maternity. As one can read in a range of equally poignant pages, for Lévinas it is not the mother but the father who, in his fecundity, generates the child—which is to say, the other whose futurity, and indeed infinity, irrupts into the present tense of egoity.

Lévinas develops the figure of paternity as fecundity in the final section of his monumental 1961 book *Totality and Infinity*. But the theme of the erotic relation, which is the premise of paternal fecundity, is already a reference to a book he wrote in the 1940s, *Existence and Existents*, as well as to some other texts from around the same time. In search of an "intersubjective relation," characterized by asymmetry and heterogeneity, Lévinas specifies the erotic relationship between the sexes as an emblematic case, writing that "intersubjectivity is the locus of transcendence in which the subject, while preserving its structure's subject, has the possibility of not inevitably returning to itself, the possibility of being fecund and (to anticipate what we shall examine later) having a son."[51] The theme he here anticipates would be realized at the end of *Totality and Infinity*, but it is worth mentioning his 1947 text anyway, since it contains an important clue. *Existence and Existents* not only explicitly thematizes sex difference; it also reveals that, as a sign of heterogeneity, sex difference perfectly serves Lévinas's argument. The sex of the subject is less explicit, in the passage in question, even though one can guess that his concern is, inevitably, the masculine gender. All the more reason for Derrida to note that *Totality and Infinity* could not have been written by a woman: "its philosophical subject is man (*vir*)."[52] The subject of which Lévinas speaks is a solipsistic I that, through eros, has the possibility of not turning fatally back upon itself; it is, as such, and with equal fatality, a virile subject.

In *Totality and Infinity*, the phenomenology of eros decidedly becomes voluptuousness and profanation and, more specifically, the carnal encounter between a male lover who "is absorbed in the complacence of the caress,"[53] and a female beloved whose being "dissipates as though into an impersonal dream without will and even without resistance, a passivity, an already animal or infantile anonymity, already entirely at death."[54] The beloved, Lévinas clarifies, "presents a face that goes beyond the face," by which he means a face that goes beyond the human: having "quit her status as a person," her "face fades, and in its impersonal and inexpressive neutrality is prolonged, in ambiguity, into animality."[55] All too recognizable, this is the well-known postulate of a coincidence, in the erotic sphere, between woman and animal—a theme on which Proudhon and Schopenhauer already had demonstrated themselves to be connoisseurs, and that finds yet another iteration in Lévinas. The interesting aspect of Lévinas's version, however, is not the fierce misogyny he inherits from the philosophical tradition and voluntarily rekindles, but rather in the way he uses this stereotype: through erotic experience, the virile subject surrenders itself to a fecundity that is just as virile. Indeed, eros here assumes the form of an occasion in which "an amorphous non-self," the female beloved, "sweeps away the I into an absolute future where it escapes itself and loses its position as a subject."[56] For the virile I to destitute itself as subject in sensual pleasures does not require it to get lost in the impersonal, dissolving itself in an ethically useless ecstasy, or unmaking its crucial *separation* from the anonymous and indistinct totality of being. It means gaining, through fecundity, the absolute future in the son—which is to say, the other of the father. And the son—like the father and unlike the female beloved—has a face. As in the case of the Woman who welcomes the I into the intimacy of the home, the patriarchal structure of Lévinas's reasoning is obvious to the point of banality. In conformity with a canon that goes back at least to Plato, Lévinas combines in these pages a misogynistic view of erotic woman with a mimetic appropriation of maternal fecundity, inserting it all into a framework characterized by patrilineal descent. "Paternity," he declares, "is a relation with a stranger who while being other . . . *is* me, a relation of the I with a self which yet is not me."[57] It is a relation with others who, although generated by the father, are neither his replica nor his repetition. Through paternity, identity, the favorite category of the Same, opens itself up to alteration. Through a fecundity that is neither pregnancy, gestation, labor, nutrition, nor care, but a generation of an other that allows the Same to open itself up to otherness, the virile I gives life to the son, and with him, to the infinity of time. The time of the father is not, in fact, the time of the son. Put in Arendtian terms: with every son, time recommences, it becomes absolute futurity, transcendence within the dimension of temporality: "the discontinuous time of fecundity makes possible an absolute youth and recommencement, while leaving the recommencement a relation with the recommenced past in a free return to that past."[58] It is precisely this discontinuous dimension of time, after all, that interests Lévinas in this section of *Totality and Infinity*. He is not interested in the son of the father as a newborn, infant, or child; even less is he interested in the son as the outcome of a biological process whose cyclical time is interrupted by the infinite temporality generated by paternal fecundity. Replaced by the father

in this theater of procreation that does not provide for any inclination, the mother is nowhere on the scene. She is notable only, if at all,
for her complete absence.

"The exteriority in which human beings show us their faces,"
writes Lévinas, "shatters the totality."[59] Compared to the speculative
totalitarianism of the I, the face of the other, in the face-to-face encounter, is a rupture, a trauma. The face of the other represents—or
better, "signifies"—a vulnerability that wounds [*vulnera*]. It wounds
the subject's compact figure and installs, in the thus-denucleated
I, the infinite and irrecusable responsibility toward the other who approaches it through the human face. Transforming into the accusative the I's nominative case, the face of the other in fact immediately
summons *me*, calling me to respond to its vulnerability, nakedness,
and indigence. It produces "an unexceptionable responsibility, preceding every free consent, every pact, every contract."[60] This summons
divests the "allegedly originary I" from its pretense of autonomy,[61]
structuring subjectivity in ethical terms as being *for-the-other* and
transforming the egoistic I into an altruistic I. It assumes different
names in Lévinas's suggestive lexicon—names that, especially beginning with his 1974 book *Otherwise Than Being*, insist on martyrdom
and self-sacrifice: election, assignment, obsession, denudation, persecution, atonement. At some points, Lévinas's writing style—abstruse
and evocative, full of ellipses, figures, metaphors, and synonyms—
risks overshadowing the essential theoretical core around which it
continues to wind itself. The fundamental thesis nevertheless remains
clear. Unlike other twentieth-century thinkers who mobilize the category of the other to enhance the effect of dissolution, Lévinas does
not divest the subject through an internal alteration that fragments,
splinters, dissolves, or consists of a "ferment of disintegration" that
involves irresponsibility.[62] He does not aim at liquidating the self
either, or at unmasking it as a mere rhetorical fiction so that nothing
remains. Like Arendt, he is convinced that God creates a "multiplicity
of dissimilarities,"[63] comprised of selves unique in their kind, and aims
instead at translating into ethical terms the human fact of uniqueness
within plurality, rooting it in the immediacy of the concrete and dual

face-to-face encounter. The uniqueness of the face of the other, by properly summoning me, elects me first of all as the responsible one who nobody else can replace. Uniqueness, Lévinas writes, here means "the impossibility of slipping away and being replaced, in which the very recurrence of the I is effected. The uniqueness of the chosen or required one, who is not a chooser, is a passivity not being converted into spontaneity. This uniqueness not assumed, not subsumed, is traumatic; it is an election in persecution."[64] Uniqueness and responsibility, provoked by the encounter with the face of the other—not the other in general but *the first to come along*—are given together in the passivity of the elected subject. This passivity is absolute: it subtracts from the concept of responsibility any initiative or choice, and negates the traditional primary role of conscience and of the subject's free will. In the egological system, Lévinas notes, "human activity, interpreted as consciousness, is always activity."[65] The identity itself is produced, surveilled, projected, and actively reinforced. "Pushed to the end," in fact, "the passivity of the elected subject "consists in inverting its identity, in getting rid of it": "the self is the passivity on the hither side of identity, that of the hostage."[66] Election, in short, inverts my identity in uniqueness. It is worth reiterating that Lévinas's ethics accords primacy to the other, to the precedence of the other over the self, proposing a relational model that could be called radical, in which the other, at the moment in which it constitutes me as unique and responsible, calls me to a never-contracted responsibility, so that "nothing is more passive than this prior questioning of all freedom."[67] With this, we are well beyond a model of relationality understood simply in terms of dependence. Put differently: in the complexity of Lévinas's outline of ethics, the face of the other is not the archetype of an originary vulnerability that characterizes humans as dependent and that implies a caring response. Rather, as he repeats in *Otherwise Than Being* and all subsequent works, the face of the persecuted transforms into the persecutor, without the persecuted ever having done any wrong, and without even knowing him or her. Lévinas's ethics is not then structured along the lines of a Hegelian drama of recognition; it is not the scene of yet another recomprehension of the Other in the Same.

Instead, my face-to-face encounter with the face of the Other summons me even before I know him or her—or better, summons me precisely because he or she is a stranger. As he writes:

> In proximity the absolutely other, the stranger whom I have "neither conceived nor given birth to," I already have on my arms, already bear, according to the Biblical formula, "in my breast as the nurse bears the nurseling." He has no other place, is not autochthonous, is uprooted, without a country, not an inhabitant, exposed to the cold and the heat of the seasons. To be reduced to having recourse to me is the homelessness or strangeness of the neighbor. It is incumbent on me.[68]

This passage is also interesting because, by using a suggestive metaphor, it allows a female figure entrusted with maternal tasks (a nurse) to reclaim an important part in the virile drama of ethics: as completely vulnerable as a nursling, Lévinas suggests here, the other is a stranger who not only regards me, but who already, as a nurse, I carry around my neck and nurture. He looms over me and persecutes me, holding me hostage. As Lisa Guenther acutely notes, in the biblical passage from which Lévinas derives his quote, the metaphor refers to a decidedly virile personage, namely Moses: he is metaphorically the nurse. In this passage, when complaining to God of having to carry the weight of the people on his shoulders, Moses says, "Did I conceive all this people? Did I bring them forth, that thou shouldst say to me, 'Carry them in your bosom, as a nurse carries the sucking child, to the land which thou didst swear to give their fathers?' Where am I to get meat to give to all this people? For they weep before me and say, 'Give us meat, that we may eat.'"[69] The feeding and carrying of the infant, in the metaphor applied to Moses, thus also refers to its conception. And even though Lévinas himself fails to mark it, the sacred text names maternity first.

In a chapter of *Otherwise Than Being*, the term *maternity* appears with notable frequency, positioned at the beginning of a lexical sequence that links it to vulnerability, responsibility, proximity, contact, and, crucially, "sensibility." Here maternity is no longer connected to the context of enjoyment and happiness but, emphatically, to that of passivity and suffering. Intent upon illustrating a proximity that is "narrower, more constrictive, than contiguity," Lévinas defines maternity as "gestation of the other in the same," and as "bearing par excellence" which "bears even responsibility for the persecuting by the persecutor."[70] He adds that maternity "binds the node of incarnation into a plot larger than the apperception of self," since "in this plot I am bound to others before being tied to my body" (which is to say, to the so-called "embodied subject").[71] This is "a plot which cannot be subordinated to the vicissitudes of representation and knowledge" because it "refers to an irrecuperable pre-ontological past," to a prebirth of the self.[72] Even though it is not easy to orient oneself in Lévinas's writing, his insistence in these pages on the self's pre-original bond with the maternal body, situating it in the realm of sensibility, amounts to yet another destitution of the sovereign subject. This was already the case in a section of *Totality and Infinity*, where, it is worth repeating, sensibility was synonymous with absolute passivity. Again, for Lévinas, the point is to observe (or, if you will, to project) the encounter with the other—here definitely understood as the other man—in the reflexive self's anterior past. In the context of the operation, Lévinas understands maternity as gestation and, not unambiguously, as carrying the other within one's one skin, thus calling maternity into question through a double meaning. On the one hand, he looks to maternity essentially as a metaphor for sensibility, as a place where the self may enter into contact with the other through sensible and passive experience, through the pre-reflexive encounter that derives from touching and caressing the other. On the other hand, perhaps letting the power of the metaphor carry him away, he also goes as far as to suggest that maternity is further confirmation that the allegedly originary self, "the inflexible ego, an undeclinable guarantee against any cancellation,"[73] is, despite its denial, originarily bound to the other—or, better still, to the female other, who carries and brings it into the world through a visceral moan. Through maternity, in other words, which in turn is connected to "the Gordian knot of the body," the ethical principle of the *for-the-other* precedes the birth of the self and characterizes it materially from the beginning. From this perspective, the future becoming hostage to the ego within the face-to-face encounter with the other—which is to say, the responsibility of the persecuted in proximity to the face of the other—thus appears as a commitment, inscribed in the very birth of the self, that it would have taken on "unbeknownst to itself."[74] We thus find a symptomatic confirmation of the other's priority over the self—an other, however, who seems to doubly besiege the self: by configuring itself both as the other to whom I am bound by my birth, in the maternal body's exemplary hospitality for the other, and as the other I encounter in the human face that summons and persecutes me, and that destitutes me as an insular self by recalling me to responsibility. The keystone of this whole construction is precisely passivity. "Maternity," for Lévinas, involves "a body suffering for another, the body as passivity and renouncement, a pure undergoing."[75] Maternity, in short, is here the exemplary case of an extreme passivity, in which the entirety of the Lévinasian ethical subject is perfectly reflected, because the face of the other calls it, without any action on its own part, to be *"for the other, despite itself."*[76]

Rereading Lévinas, and trying to recuperate his ideas on maternity from a feminist perspective, Lisa Guenther rightly notes that "both the child and the woman are in different senses vulnerable, passive, exposed to the Other."[77] While this claim is true, or at least sustainable, it nevertheless ends up highlighting even more the already noticeable absence of the child in Lévinas's pages on maternity: there is no newborn, no infant, no son. The son, it is worth recalling, appears only in the digression at the conclusion of *Totality and Infinity* on the fecundity of the father who generates him. The mother who appears in *Otherwise Than Being*, meanwhile, carries, hosts, knots, and suffers, but, however obvious or plausible it may seem to assume otherwise, the text, read to the letter, never mentions that she generates. If in the scenario of *Totality and Infinity* there is a son but not a mother, in *Otherwise* there is, perhaps, a mother but not a son. As Guenther observes, it is indeed quite significant that Lévinas uses maternity as a metaphor without connecting it to the problem of sexual difference, which he does amply discuss in other works. In this sense, although it may seem paradoxical, maternity is, for Lévinas, a gestation of the other in the same that applies to every body, or even to corporeal sensibility as such, and serves for him essentially as a way to dismantle the virile self. It is thus reasonable to doubt whether it is really worth rereading with a certain expectation Lévinas's thoughts on maternity—a maternity that, to be clear, he describes in terms of passivity, self-sacrifice, and self-abnegation, which, as Guenther writes, runs the risk of reviving "a painful and damaging cliché against which women have struggled for decades, if not centuries."[78] In truth, as far as maternity goes, Lévinas's discourse in *Otherwise* disappoints and creates discomfort. The general theoretical framework in which this disappointment grows and encysts, however, continues nevertheless to remain geometrically interesting. It is actually a framework that not only insists on a dual relationality, and is therefore "adaptable" to the scene of the mother with her child; it also, as Lévinas never tires of arguing, has the merit of highlighting the asymmetrical character of that same relation.

The face-to-face encounter with the Other, Lévinas maintains, is paradoxically but constitutively asymmetrical. The Other is not an alter ego who is identical to me; this is what individualistic ontology would want, since it places each individual, as replicas of the Same, next to one other on a horizontal plane. Equality and horizontality are typical categories for the constructions of modern egology, and in particular for the individualistic ontology that innervates the democratic model. Starting from the fact that the alterity of the Other is understood as "the Most-High" and as "the very dimension of height,"[79] Lévinasian ethics instead postulates an essential dissymmetry in the dual relation created by the epiphany of the Face. Despite the latent geometry that the term itself invokes, Lévinas understands this dissymmetry as the call of the self to a responsibility that is total, incontrovertible, without return, and that he situates as the foundation of absolute nonreciprocity. Disseminated throughout his work, this theme is developed with special clarity by Lévinas in an essay dedicated to another Jewish thinker, Martin Buber. In this short text, Lévinas expresses appreciation for Buber's account of the interhuman relation of the I-Thou encounter. In this account, the alterity of the Thou is fully preserved, and it is given as speech addressed to the ego that demands a response. This, in turn, establishes the ego as "the single person uniquely capable of responding."[80] On the other hand, however, Lévinas severely criticizes the reciprocity on which Buber insists, considering it contradictory because "without introducing a paradoxical difference of level between the I and the Thou,"[81] the alterity of the Other is lost. In an interview, Lévinas declared that "the intersubjective relation is a non-symmetrical relation," that "I am responsible for the other without waiting for reciprocity," and that the reverse is "*his* affair."[82] The encounter contains a structural imbalance, a height difference, a disparity. Assigned by the looming face of the other, my responsibility for it is total and, as it were, unilateral. There is no reciprocity—neither contextual nor ideal—only a "disparity" in which "nothing can be conceived as a correlation, that is, as a synchronization of a temporal succession, whose losses would be recuperated."[83] The fact that the Other is, in turn, responsible for me does not concern me; even less should I expect or pretend to be reciprocated: his being responsible for me or for others is precisely "his business." Even though it is provoked by the epiphany of the face of the other, Lévinasian ethics calls the I into question, not the other. Far from dissolving or disappearing from the scene, it is the I that is onstage and called into question. Uniquely responsible in this scene, and responsible because unique, the I is taken, indeed, by surprise in a relation that is unequal and deprived of reciprocity, where the face of the other charges the I with a debt it never contracted, and with a crime it never committed. Lévinas often quotes a phrase from Dostoevsky's *Brothers Karamazov*: "We are all responsible for everyone else—but I am more responsible than all the others." The Lévinasian critique of egology, far from definitively liquidating the self, clears the ground of his various philosophical prostheses so that a new I—or, better, a "me," understood in the grammar of the accusative—may emerge. This "me" has an ethical responsibility for the Other that is as peremptory and irrecusable as it is immeasurable. The dissymmetry of the face to face encounter is situated precisely in this disproportion—which, in contrast to the axiom of the principle of self-preservation, commands me imperatively to die for the other, as if the other's death were, even more than my own death, "my business."[84] While summing up his intellectual trajectory in an essay from the 1980s, Lévinas declares he thought the ethical relation "based on the face of the other, reading in its uprightness, before all mime, a defenseless exposure to the mysterious aloneness of death, and hearing in it, before all verbal expression, from the depths of that weakness, a voice that commands, an order to me signified, not to remain indifferent to that death."[85]

Death and not birth—a theme that, classically, he ignores—is the central category of Lévinas's thought. And in this sense, his ethics is, to put it in Arendtian terms, truly, as he declares, a metaphysics.[86] Ethics for him is, first of all, a lack of indifference for the other's death, or a taking responsibility for the other's death as if I were guilty of it. But ethics is also, and not by chance, my obedience to the face of the other that forbids me to kill him, prohibits me from causing his death, shedding his blood. "The entire Torah, in its minute descriptions," Lévinas argues, "is concentrated in the 'Thou Shalt not Kill' that the face of the other signifies."[87] Vulnerable, naked, defenseless, the face of the other is not just exposed to death, but to homicide, or more precisely, to murder by my hand—a murder, however, to which the face opposes an absolute resistance: "the Other is the only being that one can be tempted to kill. This temptation to murder and this impossibility of murder constitute the very vision of the face. To see a face is already to hear 'You shall not kill.'"[88] To see, to hear, to be tempted to kill while being morally unable to actually do it, are one and the same, and all come together in the face-to-face encounter. And it is precisely the *uprightness* of the other's face, who stands *in front of* me to signify that the temptation to kill is inscribed in the very event of its prohibition. As many interpreters have noted, this poses the problem of an enigmatic ambivalence within the phenomenology of the human face, whose mortality seems to be given immediately as killability, despite the equally immediate prohibition on killing. It furthermore poses the problem of the persistent use, by Lévinas, of a geometrical lexicon that is actually ill suited for his basic thesis. How indeed can one imagine in "dissymmetrical" terms a face-to-face encounter with an other who stands in front of me?

Isn't it easier to imagine a relation between two humans standing in upright posture before one another as—a symmetry? It should be added that, as Lévinas would point out, the other welcomes me in the upright-ness of his face, in a position that "is not a modification of the "along side of . . . " but is, without fail, "*direct* and *full*."[89] There hardly could be any clearer description of a disposition toward symmetric posture, even if Lévinas would decisively reject this sort of objection, accusing it of formalism. In his critique of Buber's idea of reciprocity, after hav-ing noted that the I-Thou encounter has a "formal" structure, and "can be reversed, read from left to right just as well as from right to left," Lévinas emphasizes that "in the ethics in which the other is at once higher and poorer than I, the *I* is distinguished from the *Thou*, not by any sort of 'attribute,' but by the dimension of height, which breaks with Buber's formalism."[90] And with this, two of the twentieth century's greatest Jewish thinkers diverge on the specular character of the inter-subjective relation. It is certain that, in the case of Lévinas, the problem remains unsolved because of his emphasis on height, which aggravates the problem of the structure of the encounter, at least in terms of imag-ining the face-to-face or rendering it legible. Whatever the reason that brings him to favor lemmas, figures, and tropes that are spatial—or bet-ter, geometrical—Lévinas's lexical choices produce a curious inconsis-tency with the theses they are called upon to support. Asymmetrical ethics cannot free itself, as it were, from the geometrical symmetry that illustrates it and explicates its context.

In this latent but pressing geometry, the "clues" to which are dis-seminated throughout Lévinas's opus, organized especially around terms such as *uprightness* and *height*, the category of *inclination* plays no role. This, however, isn't altogether surprising, since in the duel of ethics (the "face-to-face encounter"), neither combatant is ob-viously off-kilter or off-balance. Is it not, after all, the human body itself, which erects itself from low to high, originarily committed to the sense of Height? Is it not the I of enjoyment who is predisposed, elected, and predestined in the encounter with the face of the other, who stands before that self in the dimension of height? Even though the Face signifies the nakedness without defense of the absolutely vulnerable, the Lévinasian Other is, indeed, upright, perpendicular, erect—exactly like the I that has been awakened from its comatose egoism by the face of the other. And my responsibility for the other does not imply that I should lean over the other, that I should throw myself out of balance, that I should provide care—thus assuming the classic posture of those who, responding to the absolute vulnerability of the other, extend themselves out over the naked creature. The nakedness of the other in Lévinas, it is useful to reiterate, is not the nakedness of the newborn. Even if I already hold the other in my arms, even if I carry the other as a nurse carries an infant, the other, in the Lévinasian imaginary, still does not emphasize the figure of the infant. It summons only the figures of the orphan, the widower, and the stranger. Figures like these certainly do imply a condition of vulnerability in a particularly sharp way. But they have no relation to the scene of natality, in which precisely the newborn would be the archetype of an absolute exposure and a total nakedness.

In the inexorable chain of synonyms that Lévinas mobilizes to describe the face, which include "nakedness," "poverty," and "exposition," the term *vulnerability* has a predominant role. On the other hand, it is not a coincidence that the category of vulnerability, more than other terms, has entered into the current lexicon of contemporary philosophy inspired by Lévinas. It is therefore worth exploring it through a brief etymological digression. As Lévinas knew well, the term derives from the Latin *vulnus*, "wound," which decisively makes vulnerability a question of skin, at least according to two meanings that present a certain similarity but also a symptomatic difference. The first refers to a break in the dermis, to the traumatic laceration of the skin. Its context in the textual tradition relates to violence and war; it invokes scenarios of war, armed conflict, and violent death. Here, above all, it is warriors who wound one other, often delivering a mortal strike, trying in any case to inflict a mortal blow. This basic meaning initiates the noted semantic chain that, in modern languages, presents not only *wound* in English and *Wunde* in German, but also the Italian and Spanish verbs *ferire* and *herir* ("to wound"), both of which are attributable to the contraction of the Latin expression *vulnus inferre* ("to inflict a wound"). The *vulnus* is essentially the result of a violent blow, inflicted from the outside by a sharp instrument and with blunt force, tearing and gashing the skin. Even though the wound may extend into deep tissue, and even though is thematized essentially as lethal, the laceration pertains mainly to the epidermis, the body's limit and border, an enveloping barrier but also the surface of the body that faces toward the outside and that is therefore exposed. On the essential relation between skin and *vulnus*, however, there is also a secondary etymological conjecture that is very interesting. According to this etymology, the meaning of *vulnus*, through its root *vel*, would indicate above all skin that is smooth, hairless, and naked—skin that is, in other words, exposed to the highest degree. Words such as the Italian *vello* (sheepskin or hairy skin), and the English *avulsion* are part of this family.[91] The two etymologies, while opening up different imaginaries, are not completely in conflict: both relate to skin. But the second, avoiding the figure of the warrior, has the merit of accentuating the valence of skin as radical and immediate exposure, without covering or armor. The "vulnerable" is here the human body in its absolute nakedness, without hair, covering, or protection. The picture extends to embrace the concept of the human in general, such that the scenario of war—with its sharp instruments, but also with its protocol of symmetric violence, and its lethal outcomes—no longer appears either necessary or decisive. The warrior indeed gives way to a new emblematic figure of vulnerability as the human's essential condition: if imagined in terms of the total nakedness of the exposed skin—without hair as in the case of children and, often, of the elderly as well—the vulnerable by definition becomes, in fact, the defenseless. The warrior with his hirsute body and unkempt beard (undisputable signs of virility) resoundingly exits the scene, replaced by an archetype of the human who exposes its bare and hairless skin—to a potential wound, yes, but above all, and according to ordinary experience, to a caress, to a light touch, to cautious and trepidatious contact. The change of perspective is notable. When vulnerability is pure nakedness, when it is the defenseless who incarnates the meaning of *vulnus*, the violence that inflicts wounds slips to the background and allows for the emergence of a tender and defenseless skin that inspires caresses. Mothers and nurses, who are used to handling infants, know very well what it is like.

Lévinas, in *Totality and Infinity*, devotes a number of famous pages to the caress, which he understands as a mode of touching the vulnerable. "The caress, like contact, is sensibility. But the caress transcends the sensible. . . . The caress consists in seizing upon nothing. . . . It searches, it forages."[92] Symptomatically, Lévinas does not refer to the caress in the scene of the mother with child. He refers only to the aforementioned scene of the eros that allows the virile I, through paternal fecundity, to divest his egoity as he generates his son. In the Lévinasian lexicon, vulnerability is definitely a synonym for nudity, for exposure without defense. But this vulnerability does not find its exemplary expression in the newborn, with its tender and hairless skin, but in the face of the other, and more precisely, following a recurrent formula, in the "extreme uprightness of the face," in its "defenseless exposure," where there is "the impossibility of leaving him alone before the mystery of death."[93] Despite Derrida's perception that Lévinas's teaching on death "ran counter to the philosophical tradition extending from Plato to Heidegger,"[94] Lévinasian ethics in fact focuses on mortality, not on natality. It is true that the death Lévinas discusses is "the death of the Other, contrary to the view of contemporary philosophy, which remains attached to the self's solitary death."[95] Even so, Lévinas remains well within the speculative tradition that ignores the event of birth. Of the two etymologies of *vulnus* explored above, he ends up leaning toward the first. To simplify the argument, one could think these etymologies as two options. The first is characterized crucially by the tendency to confine the theme of vulnerability within a postulated transitivity—more a coincidence than a transition—between vulnerability, mortality, and killability. The warrior is the emblem of this option. The other insists on the paradigmatic nudity of the defenseless, and is marked instead by the capacity to generate a horizon of sense that escapes the necessity of the conceptual chain that links wound, death, and killing. With the second option, both the renowned philosophical obsession with mortality, and the corresponding warlike passion for giving and receiving violent death—exemplarily synthesized in Hobbesian theory—finally come into question. We can't neglect vulnerability's dominant etymology: here, it certainly does still indicate the wound. But it now becomes plausible that the other side of this wound would be the caress, even before death is its consequence, murder its theater. Even though Lévinas tends to emphasize *vulnus* as laceration rather than caress, the mode in which he conceptualizes vulnerability oscillates ambiguously between the two options. His thought on this theme, in other words, is traversed by internal tensions that give rise, at the very least, to a double register. The register that attributes vulnerability to a phenomenology of the skin is in fact accompanied by another register, one that is, as it were, more traditional, which instead attributes vulnerability to a thematic of mortality and killing. In the first option, vulnerability is decisively bare skin, "the extremities in which [the body] begins and ends," subjectivity as sensibility, exposure to others, responsibility in the proximity of the other, "as an obsession by the other, or a maternity."[96] Here Lévinas's accent is on contact and openness, on a constitutive and unintentional exposure to the other, according to the figure of an an-archic and pre-originary relation. This is, then, a vulnerability that emphasizes ethical responsibility (or that even, if you will, postulates a radical relational ontology) without the themes of mortality or homicide necessarily entering the picture. Obviously, it is always present in Lévinas's mind that man is mortal and that defenseless creatures (such as orphans, widows, and strangers) are more exposed than others to the wound and to violent death. But the original trait of his version of vulnerability consists precisely in his ability, or at least attempt, to escape from this logic. This is why he thinks in terms of a relationality that exposes the one to the other, and that summons ethical responsibility beyond death and murder, beyond violence and aggression. In these cases, the etymology of *vulnus* as nudity prevails over the etymology of *vulnus* as laceration. More than the potentially lethal wound, what prevails here is the skin's nudity, sensibility, contact. It is worth repeating that this meaning of vulnerability as exposure of the one to the other, which is removed from the *primum logicum* of violence—and assumed instead in terms of absolute hospitality, welcoming, and abode—is often related by Lévinas to "feminine being" and the "dimension of femininity." Even though Lévinas's vision of woman and maternity takes the shape of yet another homage to classical androcentrism, it is nevertheless possible to argue that, at times, his thinking moves within a framework that tries to release the category of vulnerability from a bellicose and virilist imagery.

In another framework, which perhaps prevails in Lévinasian reflection, the register, precisely, changes. In this version, "pure vulnerability" coincides essentially with exposure to death, if not to violent death and homicide. Even though the accent always falls on the immediate expression of the other's face, which is naked, defenseless, and unshielded, Lévinas pays special attention, within the face-to-face encounter, to the skin "exposed to wound and outrage."[97] Here it is definitively death that signifies the ethical summons, peremptory and irresistible, of the face. "Such is the face as the very *mortality* of the other person,"[98] Lévinas writes. However—and this is undoubtedly the most critical point—the face is also what evokes the temptation of homicide, by commanding, "Thou shalt not kill." The vulnerable, the mortal, and the killable thus return and are inscribed in a single, traditional chain—which, in truth, is now broken by a phenomenology of the Face that provokes homicidal temptation even as it also prohibits it. There is a passage by Lévinas, which has been reflected upon by Judith Butler among others, that illustrates a problematic side to the prohibition to kill, which paradoxically coexists and overlaps with the temptation to kill. In this minor text, which refers to Rabbi Rachi's commentary on chapter 32 of Genesis, Lévinas meditates on the story of Jacob, who, when hearing that his brother Esau is marching against him "at the head of four hundred men," is afraid that he may die, yes, but above all is anguished that he may have to kill.[99] For Lévinas, this anguish, which is capable of prevailing over the ego's drive to survive, is already an effect of the command "thou shalt not kill," which is expressed by the face of the other in the encounter between two unique beings who gaze upon one other "face-to-face." In the "face-to-face" encounter, moreover, there is no longer an I characterized by the *conatus essendi*, a selfish and possessive I, but an I, a *me*, that already has been dispossessed by the "thou shalt not kill" that is expressed by the face of the other, which precisely constitutes me through this "thou." However, some perplexities arise when we consider that it is homicide, or if you will the temptation to commit homicide—understood as simultaneous with the prohibition of killing—that enacts the dynamics which, in turn, constitute the *me* through the "thou." Here, in fact, we witness the symptomatic and unresolved overlap of the two registers, of the two Lévinasian versions of the vulnerable outlined above. We see how violence continues to have an effect on the first register, which is quite prevalent in Lévinas's thought, and which contains the "thou shalt not kill" even as it prohibits, opposes, and curses violence, with the result that the belligerent, sovereign, and aggressive subject continues to return like a specter (at the very least). In the second register, meanwhile, which is marked by a phenomenology of the skin as nudity, and which appears only sporadically in Lévinas's texts, violence seems to give up its domain, leaving the scene to a nude and defenseless face that announces the humanity of man in the terms of a primary vulnerability that precedes the eventuality of injury. Sensitive to this theme and to its treatment by Lévinas, Butler reminds us that "it is important to note here that Lévinas is not saying that primary relations are abusive or terrible; he is simply saying that at the most primary level we are acted upon by others in ways over which we have no say, and that this passivity, susceptibility, and condition of *being impinged upon* inaugurate who we are."[100] Even if Butler's emphasis is on the "inaugural impingement" that supposedly characterizes the scene of birth and infancy, the overlapping of the two registers, with the inevitable prevalence of the connection between vulnerability and killability, thus also influences Butler's recuperation of Lévinasian ethics. However questionable this recuperation may be, in terms of our commentary it really hits the mark. In Lévinas's conception of ethics, which insists especially on asymmetry, it is in fact difficult to model the face of the Other on Esau's physiognomy: the brother in arms, as the figure of a symmetry between warriors and brothers, is rather dubious not just for an asymmetrical ethics but also for any authentic foundation of peace. Here the latent geometry definitely has the upper hand. It is, moreover, worth mentioning that the name Esau, which in Hebrew means "hairy" or "hirsute"—the hunter Esau by now had already been tricked out of his primogeniture by the hairless Jacob—seems at the very least to be unsuitable to invoke the theme of vulnerability. Many aspects in fact make the Lévinasian use of this biblical story quite problematic, as if there were already a serious difficulty, even danger, in resorting to examples to illustrate the non-conceptualizable and irrepresentable ethics of the "for the Other."

The face, Lévinas declares, is abstract: "the epiphany of the Other involves a signifyingness of its own, independent of this meaning received from the world. The Other comes to us not only out of context but also without mediation; he signifies by himself."[101] The face, in other words, signifies in its nudity. Despite the extraordinary polyvalence of the term "nudity" within the Lévinasian lexicon, this in fact remains, in the last analysis, its fundamental meaning: absolute exposure, without masks or interference or references, without the mediation of context, just nude, direct, and abstract. Nudity and abstraction are, in this sense, synonyms within the vocabulary of Lévinas, such that when abstraction is applied to the face, it assumes a meaning all its own. Contrary to the traditional philosophical lexicon, the abstract in this case does not refer to the operation of abstracting from the particular to produce the universal; nor does it mean the opposite of concrete. The face is abstract, Lévinas says, because its self-signification abstracts precisely from context—which is to say from the world, from the frames of meaning shared by different historical or empirical situations, and not least from language itself. The face, then, has no attributes or qualities. If, to simplify the discussion, we were to translate Lévinas's lexicon into Arendt's, we would say that the face signifies the other's singularity implied by the question "*Who* is he?" whereas the question "*What* is he?"—because it relates to context, qualities and attributes—remains offstage and immaterial for ethics. If anything, were this question to interfere with the face-to-face encounter, it would

impair its expressiveness. From this perspective, the widow and the orphan Lévinas often calls upon, not to mention the foreigner, the poor,
and the stateless, are all undue interferences, a window onto worldly
matters that ends up disturbing the nudity and abstraction of the face's
own signification. Even more disturbing is his reference to the story of
Esau and Jacob, or other stories from the Book of Books. The habit
of Talmudic commentary and to its type of narrative, symptomatically
leads him to transgress his own thesis when he contextualizes the face.
Any qualification or specification that inserts the face into a social or
cultural context, or even into a certain value system or a particular
narration, amounts only to a superfluous silhouette, adding nothing to
the face but an unnecessary contour and an often pathetic accent. But,
according to Lévinas, it is precisely the pathetic that should stay strictly
off-scene! For him, it is worth emphasizing, the nudity of the other
does not become more naked because the other is an orphan without
clothing or a poor man trembling in his rags. Nudity and abstraction
coincide in the face of the other precisely because they are unrelated to
the encounter's contingent circumstances: no social or cultural identity dresses up the face that self-signifies, directly and peremptorily, in
front, face-to-face, without any mediation. No context is necessary for
the absolute and irrevocable responsibility commanded by the extreme
uprightness of the face of the other, defenseless and exposed to death,
whatever its history or situation might be. The face of the other elects
me to a position of total altruism, which far from being dependent on
circumstances, derives from precisely this abstraction.

Unique in its naked signification, the face summons me and commands me not to kill, emerging from a theater without backdrop.
The ethical relation is abstract, not because it relies on general formulas or universal principles, but because it excludes all effects issu-
ing from the specificity of a given context. The problem is that, even
though Lévinas is convinced of the importance of this thesis, and
indeed hardly misses a chance to reiterate it, his own writing ends
up regularly disproving it. When he writes about the "face-to-face"
encounter, he continually invokes the orphan, the widower, and the
stranger, as well as the poor, the indigent, the hungry, the stateless or

even episodes taken from the repertoire of the Torah. In short, despite his insistence on the abstraction of the face, Lévinas nevertheless does not at all give up contextualizing the ethical relation, indeed even in terms that are often pathetic, whether by borrowing stylized motifs from the Bible or, more simply, by situating it in exemplary cases or in circumstances related to ordinary experience or common life. This brings to light, if not a contradiction internal to his thought, at least some interesting issues that are worthy of special consideration.

One of these, which Lévinas mentions in passing in a brief response to an interview question, surprisingly regards the relation of mother to child and, in particular, the exemplarity of maternal altruism. Inserted within a critique of Heidegger and his theory of *Befindlichkeit* (affectivity),[102] Lévinas's argument concerns the capacity of the I to shed its selfishness and worry for the other instead of itself—to be anguished for the other's death without also imagining itself in the same situation, hence without also being afraid, indeed, for its own death. To illustrate his thesis and to diminish its apparently scandalous quality, or, if you will, to make it credible or even familiar, Lévinas uses two examples. He first mentions "the mother who fears for the child" and "each of us who fears for their friends." He then adds, with a wink to the interviewer, "But every 'other man' is a friend. Do you see what I mean?"[103] As an expert reader of Lévinas, the interviewer probably did in fact see what he meant, but given the questionable equivalence of the two examples Lévinas gave, it is a bit doubtful that even he was satisfied with Lévinas's explanation. It is not hard to see, at the level of exemplary efficacy, a significant difference between the mother who fears for her child and each of us who fears for our friends. The first example is immediately clear and convincing: the mother afraid for her child, and the theme of fearing for the child's death more than for her own, is a phenomenon that is so well known, so taken for granted, that it is hardly in need of any additional arguments. Whether or not this is a stereotype, whether it is natural or culturally produced, it is a given that pertains both to ordinary experience and to common feeling, an indisputable fact that belongs to the order of reality. And it is precisely for this reason that the mother's fear for her child can indeed function as an efficacious example of the very total altruism—boundless and sacrificial—that, here as elsewhere, Lévinas theorizes. The same cannot be said, however, about each of us fearing for a friend's death more than for our own: this is a rare case that is more speculative than realistic, more theoretical than practical, and in any case is unworkable as an example if its purpose is to illustrate and prove the difficult thesis that Lévinas sustains. This, indeed, is a thesis that, as Lévinas knows, encounters serious difficulties that must be absorbed and overcome; above all, it is very hard to prove with convincing examples from common experience. When, really, do we ever fear our friend's death more than our own? This, in other words, is a thesis that, if brought down into ordinary life, risks appearing abstract in the traditional sense. Lévinas himself admits that one could be "scandalized by this utopian and, for a self, inhuman conception,"[104] and by this absolute altruism in which the other's death concerns me more than my own. He also admits that his writing condenses the sense of ethics in "extreme formulas" that are not easily translatable into realistic terms.[105] All the more reason that the example of the mother fearing for her child should appear precious to him, since it clearly is incomparable with the example of the friend who is afraid for his friend. What "love without concupiscence," to use Lévinas's words,[106] could in fact break from the axiom of the sovereign selfishness, if not a mother's love for her child? What other image of radical altruism could serve as a better example, while also remaining familiar and credible? What infinite responsibility for the other could lower itself, in spite of the self, to lower itself into a more docile hostage? What subjectivity, which figure or character or theme from the real world, could compete with this?

"I speak of responsibility," Lévinas declares, "as the essential, primary and fundamental structure of subjectivity. For I describe subjectivity in ethical terms. Ethics, here, does not supplement a preceding existential base; the very node of the subjective is knotted in ethics understood as responsibility."[107] If the autonomous, sovereign, and solipsistic I is the subject that has been inhabiting the history of ontology for centuries, then Lévinasian ethical subjectivity constitutes itself "in the very movement wherein being responsible for the other devolves on it."[108] Or, put into a formula: "subjectivity as such is initially hostage."[109] Derrida similarly speaks of "the constitution of subjectivity in subjection, in being subjected, in subjectivation."[110] The idea behind this formula is not new; it stands out in Foucault's opus and marks in various ways the entire poststructuralist season, as Derrida certainly knows. Lévinas, however, gives it a different and peculiar twist. The most original part of Lévinas's proposal is precisely in the structural bond between ethics and subjectivity, a point upon which he often insists and which he uses as an essential principle to critically revisit, in an indubitably radical way, both the question of ethics and that of the subject. Stated differently, Lévinas's thesis on the ethical movement of subjectivization, which aims at connecting the singularity of the *elected* with the irrecusable responsibility that subjects the self despite itself, exceeds in its disruptiveness and depth all other critiques of the subject developed in France during the second half of the twentieth century. Many readers still find it especially original and convincing. Many of these same readers, however, have been less convinced by Lévinas's notorious attempt to take a further step, and to make a connection between ethics and politics. And for good reason: this is perhaps the weakest point of Lévinas's whole speculative system, one that the author of *Otherwise Than Being* never completely resolved. To quote one of his very best readers, Francesco Paolo Ciglia, "the problem of the foundation or justification of the political dimension is, in fact, one of the most pressing and tormenting theoretical concerns on which Lévinas meditates in his later work."[111] Not least because of the various critiques that have been leveled at Lévinas on this point, and because of his consequent reactions, revisions, and clarifications, the question has grown in complexity. At the risk of oversimplifying it, I will attempt now to summarize that question in a schematic way by returning to the interview discussed above.

Stated concisely, the keystone of the Lévinasian theory of the link between ethics and politics is the category of the "third." According to Lévinas, politics, which he mostly summarizes under the rubric of "justice," comes into play when a "third" is added to the dual relation between me and the other (from which the sense of ethics originates). This "third" is the neighbor of the neighbor, the other of the other, or in short, "the fact of the multiplicity of men and the presence of someone else next to the Other."[112] The third, for Lévinas, is thus a question of numbers or, if you will, of quantity, which, in turn, is symptomatic of the ancient question—inaugurated by Plato, and then taken up by the entire history of philosophy—of the relation between the one and the many. Lévinas reclaims this question in terms—equally Platonic, after all—of the transition from duality to multiplicity by way of the figure of the "third." It is worth reiterating that Lévinasian ethics consists structurally of a dyadic relationship that is characterized by a certain spatial configuration: the I and the other, face-to-face with and in front of one another. But, as Lévinas is forced to admit, the world is comprised, not of a series of duets, or duels, but of a plurality of human beings who, far from confronting one another face-to-face, and instead much more plausibly, stand beside each other, side-by-side with one another. While trying to summarize in an interview his idea of politics, Lévinas said: "If I am alone with the Other, I owe him everything; but there is someone else. Do I know what my neighbor is in relation to someone else? . . . The interpersonal relation I establish with the Other, I must also establish with other man; there is thus a necessity to moderate this privilege of the Other; from whence comes justice. Justice, exercised through institutions, which are inevitable, must always be held in check by the initial interpersonal relation."[113]

What Lévinas registers here is precisely that, besides the two, the I and the other, there is also the "third," and, by multiplication, innumerable others. The *one* so dear to Plato never enters the picture: the problem of the connection between ethics and politics, for Lévinas, is configured as a transition from duality to plurality—or, more precisely, from an ethical and subjectivizing relation between two who face one another, to a social relation among many who do not look one another in the face. This is far from a minor transition, since in the political dimension, which is to say in the sphere of "inevitable" institutions, there is now a new need "to weigh, to think, to judge, in comparing the incomparable."[114] This promises to be quite a difficult task, both because it is not possible for "singular" beings to be evaluated, thought, and judged, and because between the ethical and the political realms there is—despite Lévinas's claims to the contrary—an unbridgeable gap, a lethal leap, an incomparability. From the structure of the ethical relation, which he describes as asymmetrical and unequal, and which remains the foundation of the whole operation (its genetic principle and criterion), he transitions to the egalitarian structure of the paradigm of the modern state, a historical model he engages with by calling into question—and this is worth noticing—not its form, namely the general principle of . . . , but only its natural law premise (especially in Hobbes's violent anthropology). In the Lévinasian construction, the transition consists in moving from the very first and fundamental form of sociality, the dual face-to-face encounter, to the second but inevitable form of sociality exercised by democratic institutions. The latter must remain accountable to the former and, as he says, preserve its memory: not only does the second form of sociality derive from the first, but it is also constitutively overshadowed by it.[115] Lévinas is aware of the equivocality of the conceptual structure of his argument. In order to prevent the political outcome of his quite original thesis on the ethical subjectivity of *uniqueness* from being understood as an endorsement of the much less original modern individualistic ontology of *identity* and *repetition*, Lévinas alludes to Hobbes's famous formula *homo homini lupus*: "It is not unimportant to know—and this is perhaps the European experience of the twentieth century—whether the egalitarian and just State in which the European realizes himself—and that is to be instituted and preserved—proceeds from a war of all against all—or from the irreducible responsibility of one for the other, and whether it can ignore the uniqueness of the face and of love."[116] In other words:

> It is extremely important to know if society in the current sense of the term is the result of a limitation of the principle that men are predators of one another, or if to the contrary it results from the limitation of the principle that men are *for* one another. Does the social, with its institutions, universal forms and laws, result from limiting the conse-

quences of the war between men, or from limiting the infinity which opens in the ethical relationship of man to man?[117]

According to Lévinas, therefore, the task of politics is to limit the ethical opening to the infinite, not to limit the postulated natural war of all against all. The alternative he proposes, which has the capacity of interrogating the foundations of modern political thought, is in effect drastic: there is a crucial difference between thinking that the "just and egalitarian State" is premised on a selfish, warlike, and sovereign subject (as described by Hobbes), or on an altruistic subject, which is moved by a love without concupiscence and is, as such, pacifist (as described in Lévinasian ethics). Beyond his unsatisfying conception of the meaning of politics, the change of perspective he suggests is in fact remarkable, subversive, and radical. First of all, Lévinas counteracts modernity's hegemonic tendency to separate ethics from politics, retying them tightly into a knot that affirms the foundational role and primacy of ethics. Secondly, but not less importantly, Lévinas breaks the fatal bond between politics and war that traditional philosophy thought unbreakable, daring to postulate that, *in principio*, there is peace. It is no accident that the object of his critique is Hobbes, and not a blander version of the construction of statual political order, based on a vision of man that is less violent and aggressive (as we find, for example, in Locke and in liberal doctrine more generally). With an intentionally outdated, provocative, and minoritarian choice, Lévinas opposes precisely the political *realism* of political analysis for which Hobbesian discourse, in many ways and in many schools of twentieth-century thought, has become an exemplary paradigm—a paradigm that remains very popular and much appreciated even today, having achieved the status of a guarantee of the objectivity of any "scientific discourse" on politics. In this sense, Lévinas is one of the few exponents of contemporary thought who has defied the protocols of political anthropology that prescribe realism as a synonym for epistemic correctness. Against any rhetoric that postulates violence as rationally necessary, he dares to propose an absolute and radical pacifism. Stated as a formula: for Lévinas, politics is the continuation, by other means, of the ban on killing. This continuation presupposes "a sensibility in which the scandal of murder is not suppressed even when the violence is rationally necessary."[118]

In light of this radicalism, it is even more surprising that Lévinas was not more resolute in attacking "the roots" of the verticalist model underlying the structure of modern politics and individualistic ontology. The signs of this failure are, unfortunately, not hard to find. The face-to-face relation implies a postural geometry that seems to announce the usual and suspect symmetry—which is to say, the same fateful symmetry that, despite Lévinas's claims to the contrary, is synonymous with equality and remains an indispensable category for the European state (which hardly has renounced the theory of the social contract, up to and including Hobbes's). It is at least curious that the two forms of sociality that Lévinas contemplates—the dual relation of ethics, and the plural relation of politics, which preserves the latter's memory—both allow their protagonists to remain standing in their upright posture, joined on account of their common and prejudicial subscription to the paradigm of verticality. Tellingly, neither the dimension of *height* opened up by the face of the other nor the *rectitude* of the other's gaze that, straight like an arrow and without deviation, hits me in the face, can be said to be geometrically novel or disruptive: instead, despite their radicalness, both, in the last analysis, replicate the Cartesian axes quite explicitly. For this reason, one can hardly say that the Lévinasian philosophy brings forth any geometrical breakthrough. From this point of view, Walter Benjamin's fragment—with which we opened this book—appears much more promising. Lévinas, by contrast, lets inclination escape the grip of ethics and of the subjectivizing movement it brings forth.

After all, it is very important that the subjectivizing movement, the constitution of subjectivity in the subjection of the hostage, comes from a face belonging to an other who is exposed without defense to death. Stated differently, it is very significant that the classical theme of death also affects Lévinas's discourse on the ethical construction of subjectivity, whatever the anomalies such a discourse may otherwise include. Indeed, this same problem may be detected in a substantial ambiguity structuring his entire conceptualization. On the one hand, the face of the other, irremediably exposed and abandoned to death, seems to hint at the simple fact of human mortality—at our awareness of being mortal. Lévinas's concern with mortality, however, does not call upon the traditional reaction against death of the *conatus essendi* so dear to modern philosophy; it instead assumes the form of a passive and irresistible abandonment. On the other hand, the temptation to kill, which is suggested by the face of the other at the same time that it prohibits it, decidedly invokes violent death and the extreme act of murder. This situation poses a serious problem: there is a fundamental difference between death thematized as natural and inevitable (its inscrutability and mystery notwithstanding) and death thematized as violent and premature (inflicted by a human hand). In the first case, it is conceivable on Lévinas's terms that the responsibility of the hostage for the other's death could be configured as a form of love without concupiscence. In the second case, however, a configuration of this sort is rather hard to conceive. Between natural death and violent death, as Hobbes well knew, there is an essential and unbridgeable gap. It is thus worth asking if the classical philosophical theme of death, albeit treated from a different angle, is indeed the most appropriate for rethinking politics and its anthropological presuppositions in terms of peace instead of war. One could ask if the Arendtian gesture of shifting focus from death to birth, accompanied by a reconsideration of maternal inclination, wouldn't be a better move. The idea of a peace that situates itself *in principio*, which is to say the daring thesis of an ethical and anthropological foundation for peace, needs an imaginary completely apart from geometrical verticalism. To insist upon uprightness and height does not offer much hope in this regard. More hopeful is the hypothesis that finds the imaginary resources for pacifism residing in the face of the mother inclined over her child—which, not by chance, is often represented in art as elusive and enigmatic.

IN THE PAINTING BY LEONARDO we considered earlier, *The Virgin and Child with St. Anne*, Mary and the Christ child look at each other face to face. Mary's inclination toward the child also signals the curved line along which her gaze meets the child's, whose face is in turn is reclined backward relative to his body so that it can meet his mother's eyes. Even if the lamb he embraces symbolizes the future Passion of Christ, Mary's face almost shows a smile; she is anxious but also serene in her melancholy. The same can be said of many of the representations of the Virgin Mary with Child, depicted by countless artists across the centuries. In the face of the Mother portrayed by Christianity, however aching or melancholic or invaded by tenderness it may be, there are nevertheless enigmatic traits of intense and detached serenity, which frequently are positioned as the exemplary expression of love without concupiscence—without further purpose, without any ambition to possess or any anxiety of control, satisfied in its sublime composure. In the various versions of this pictorial theme, Mary sometimes looks at her child, at other times gazes at us, and at still others seems to see an infinite point on the horizon, which makes her expression even more enigmatic—serene but disquieting. Perhaps it is not by chance that a face of peace figured in feminine features should assume the form of an enigma—but also a promise, one that is all too familiar yet still unknown, that needs to be actualized, a stereotypical altruism that needs to be rethought and reinterrogated. There is, after all, a type of altruism that is not abnegation and martyrdom, suffering, and renunciation and that does not require a privileged connection with the horizon of death (as Lévinas, like so many others, would prefer). Right at the heart of the self-sacrificing stereotype—right there where patriarchalism seems once again to triumph—there is a form of altruism that presents itself as unusual, problematic, even unheard of, but all the same tangible in the detached and serene smile of Leonardo's Madonna. It is as if the Mother's posture called us to a prosaic and mundane serenity, which her gesture in turn visually narrates: an active inclination to place the child on her lap before the equally serene and pleased gaze of Anne (who, with hand on hip, adds a note of familiarity to the image). If this altruism is exemplary, then it is characterized by a sure and practical love, so everyday and spontaneous that it does not express signs of suffering or self-sacrifice, and even less of excessive self-awareness. Perhaps this is the source of the ambiguity of the smiles of so many

Renaissance Madonnas: keepers of a gift that is larger than life itself, larger even than the very idea of God, they seem only marginally aware of its magnitude, although they perceive its perturbing effect and perhaps even enjoy it. The ambiguity of their smile seems to hint at the secret peace that gift carries, which needs neither glorious scenarios with which to celebrate its magnitude nor extreme achievements to verify its significance. Even less does this gift need vertical lines lifting it above the world and its bodies. In the final analysis, the smile and inclination of Leonardo's Mother suggests that there is a carnal sense of existence, as mundane as it is prosaic, that consists primarily in her irrevocable inclination toward the other—which is there in plain sight for all to see, yet hidden to the ennobling eye of theory. The Mother's posture is oblique in precisely the same way that her smile is; the clues to her secret, like so many Renaissance enigmas, are so obvious that they have remained altogether invisible to the preoccupied gaze of the intellect.

Notes

Introduction

Epigraph: Niccolò Tommaseo, *Nuovo dizionario dei sinonimi della lingua italiana* (Florence: Luigi Pezzati, 1830).

1. Walter Benjamin, *Gesammelte Schriften*, vol. 6, ed. Rolf Tiedemann and Hermann Schweppenhäuser (Frankfurt: Suhrkamp, 1974–99), p. 55. For an elaborate interpretation of the fragment, see Brendan Moran, "Eros Thanatos in Benjamin's Goethe's Elective Affinities," in *The Erotic: Approaches to a Cultural Contextualisation*, ed. Koen De Temmerman (Oxford: Inter-Disciplinary-Press, 2005), pp. 1–5.

2. [In the few cases where Cavarero's engagement with the discourse of rectitude risks being obscured by the available English equivalents, we have included Cavarero's Italian in brackets.—Trans.]

3. These are the first two definitions of *inclinazione* in the *Grande dizionario della lingua italiana*, ed. Salvatore Battaglia (Turin: Unione Tipografico-Editrice Torinese, 1961). The majority of dictionaries of modern western languages opt for a similar choice for *inclination* in English and French, although the latter includes the variant *inclinaison* in the scientific field, *inclinaciòn* in Spanish, and *Neigung* in German.

4. Immanuel Kant, *Lectures on Ethics*, ed. Peter Heath and J. B. Schneewind, trans. Peter Heath (Cambridge: Cambridge University Press, 2001), p. 177.

5. Plato, *Laws* 847a, trans. A. E. Taylor, in *The Collected Dialogues of Plato*, ed. Edith Hamilton and Huntington Cairns (New York: Pantheon Books, 1961).

6. Pierre-Joseph Proudhon, *La pornacratie, ou les femmes dans les temps modernes* (Antony, France: Tops-H. Trinquier, 2013), p. 177. [Trans. by the translators of this volume.]

7. Arthur Schopenhauer, *Essays of Schopenhauer*, trans. Mrs. Rudolf Dircks (London: Walter Scott, 1900), p. 65.

8. Hannah Arendt, "Some Questions of Moral Philosophy," in *Responsibility and Judgment*, ed. Jerome Kohn (New York: Schocken, 2003), p. 81.

9. [The Italian *io*, like the German *Ich*, can refer to the "self" or "ego" as well as to the use of the first-person singular pronoun "I." Cavarero's critique of the *io* of modern philosophy not only uses these two senses interchangeably and simultaneously (so that her references to "self" or "ego" are also, and at the same time, references to the use of the first-person singular pronoun, and vice versa); it also extends to include the very appearance of the pronoun *I* itself, the rectilinear typography of which testifies to its exemplary place and function within the discourse of "rectitude." Our translations of *io* have observed the distinction in English grammar between the nouns "self" and "ego," on the one hand, and the pronoun "I," on the other: depending on the requirements of the sentence and paragraph in question, as well as the text Cavarero is interpreting, we have at some points rendered *io* as "self" or "ego," and at other points as "I" or even "the I" (most especially in Chapter 3 and the Coda, where the relevant extant English texts authorize and even require this construction). The reader, however, should bear in mind that these distinctions do not hold for Cavarero, who to the contrary seeks throughout this book to critique a genre of the self, a formation of the ego, or a mode of subjectivation that actualizes itself grammatically in and through the utterance of an upright, independent, and rectilinear "I."—Trans.]

10. Arendt, "Some Questions of Moral Philosophy," p. 81.

11. María Zambrano, *Sentimenti per un'autobiografia: Nascita, amore, pietà*, ed. Samantha Maruzzella (Milan: Mimesis, 2012), p. 58.

12. Marcel Proust, *Swann's Way*, trans. Lydia Davis (New York: Penguin, 2002), p. 244.

13. Ibid., pp. 247–48.

14. Leo Tolstoy, *Anna Karenina: A Novel in Eight Parts*, trans. Richard Pevear and Larissa Volokhonsky (New York: Penguin, 2002), pp. 763–64.

15. Ibid., p. 315.

16. Ibid., p. 695.

17. Marina Warner, *Alone of All Her Sex: The Myth and the Cult of the Virgin Mary* (London: Vintage, 1983), p. 336.

18. Simone de Beauvoir, *The Second Sex*, trans. Constance Borde and Sheila Malovany-Chevallier (New York: Vintage, 2011), p. 5.

19. Jonas expressed this judgment, in a confidential tone, in an April 19, 1980, letter to Günther Anders, Arendt's first husband. Cited in Christian Dries, "Günther Anders und Hannah Arendt, eine Beziehungsskizze," in Günther

Anders, *Die Kirschenschlacht: Dialoge mit Hannah Arendt und ein akademisches Nachwort*, ed. Gerhard Oberschlick (Munich: C. H. Beck, 2011), p. 105. [Trans. by the translators of this volume.]

20. Ann V. Murphy, "Corporeal Vulnerability and New Humanism," *Hypatia*, 26:3 (2011): 575–90.

21. Emmanuel Lévinas, *Proper Names*, trans. Michael B. Smith (Stanford, CA: Stanford University Press, 1996), p. 19.

22. Emmanuel Lévinas, *Totality and Infinity: An Essay on Exteriority*, trans. Alphonso Lingis (Norwell, MA: Kluwer Academic, 1991), p. 23.

23. Judith Butler, *Precarious Life: The Powers of Mourning and Violence* (London: Verso, 2004), p. 24.

Chapter 1: Adam's Line

Epigraph: Walt Whitman, *Democratic Vistas* (New York: J. S. Redfield, 1871).

1. Heinrich Krauss, *Il Paradiso: Storia e cultura*, trans. Michaela Mastroddi (Rome: Donzelli, 2005), p. 32. ["The man named his wife 'Eve' because she was the mother of all those who live" (Genesis 3:20).—Trans.]

2. [The Italian noun *uomo*, like the English noun *man*, can signify both the "human being" in general and the "adult male" in particular. Here, as elsewhere (e.g., Chapter 8), Cavarero uses the term *uomo* to mark the way in which received concepts of the human derive their sense from implicitly gendered schemata.—Trans.]

3. John Locke, *Two Treatises of Government: And a Letter Concerning Toleration*, ed. Ian Shapiro (New Haven, CT: Yale University Press, 2003), p. 123.

4. Ibid.

5. Ibid.

6. Ibid., p. 126.

7. Ibid., p. 122.

8. Ibid., p. 135.

9. Ibid., p. 127.

Chapter 2: Kant and the Newborn

First epigraph: Fyodor Dostoevsky, *The Adolescent*, trans. Richard Pevear and Larissa Volokhonsky (New York: Vintage, 2003), p. 71.
Second epigraph: Friedrich Nietzsche, "On the Genealogy of Morals," trans. Walter Kaufmann and R. J. Hollingdale, in *On The Genealogy of Morals / Ecce Homo*, ed. Walter Kaufmann (New York: Vintage, 1989), p. 107.

1. Immanuel Kant, "Conjectures on the Beginning of Human History," in *Political Writings*, ed. Hans Reiss, trans. H. B. Nisbet (Cambridge: Cambridge University Press, 1991), p. 222.

2. Miguel de Unamuno, *The Tragic Sense of Life in Men and Nations*, trans. Anthony Kerrigan (Princeton, NJ: Princeton University Press, 1972), p. 6.

3. Kant, "Conjectures on the Beginning of Human History," 222.

4. Immanuel Kant, *Anthropology from a Pragmatic Point of View*, trans. and ed. Robert B. Louden (Cambridge: Cambridge University Press, 2006), p. 16.

5. Ibid. [Translation modified.—Trans.]

6. Immanuel Kant, "Groundwork of The Metaphysics of Morals," in *Practical Philosophy*, trans. and ed. Mary Gregor (Cambridge: Cambridge University Press, 1996), pp. 98–101.

7. Kant, *Anthropology*, p. 159.

8. Ibid., p. 40.

9. Ibid.; emphasis in original.

10. Ibid., p. 149.

11. Ibid., p. 168.

12. Ibid., p. 168 n. d.

13. [The Italian phrase here, "una creatura inerme e dipendente," is worthy of the reader's attention. Although in ordinary language the adjective *inerme* can be translated either as "helpless" or "defenseless," it is something a term of art in Cavarero's thought, and as such we have translated it in this book exclusively as "defenseless."—Trans.]

14. Tzvetan Todorov, *Life in Common: An Essay in General Anthropology*, trans. Katherine Golsan and Lucy Golsan (Lincoln: University of Nebraska Press, 2001), pp. 5–6.

15. G. W. F. Hegel, *Philosophy of Mind: Being Part Three of the "Encyclopædia of the Philosophical Sciences" (1830)*, trans. William Wallace and A. V. Miller (Oxford: Clarendon, 1971), p. 58.

16. Ibid., pp. 58–59.

17. Kant, *Anthropology*, p. 168.

18. Todorov, *Life in Common*, p. 43.

19. Davide Tarizzo, *La vita: Un'invenzione recente* (Rome: Laterza, 2010), p. 7. [Trans. by the translators of this volume.] Tarizzo develops an innovative analysis of the importance of the concept of autonomy in Kant, see in particular pp. 3–35.

20. Michel Foucault, *Introduction to Kant's Anthropology*, trans. Roberto Nigro and Kate Briggs (Los Angeles: Semiotext[e], 2008), p. 50.

21. On Kant, infants, and their "obscure idea" of freedom, see Tommaso Tuppini, "Kant, Blows of Tears," in *Kant's Philosophy of the Unconscious*, trans. Piero Giordanetti, Riccardo Pozzo, and Marco Sgarbi (Berlin: De Gruyter, 2012), pp. 148–76.

22. Hannah Arendt, *Denktagebuch: 1950 bis 1973*, ed. Ursula Ludz und Ingeborg Nordmann (Munich: Piper, 2002), p. 818. [Trans. by the translators of this volume; emphasis in original.]

23. Ibid., p. 775. [Trans. by the translators of this volume.]

24. Hannah Arendt, "Some Questions of Moral Philosophy," in *Responsibility and Judgment*, ed. Jerome Kohn (New York: Schocken, 2003), p. 81.

25. Ibid., p. 68.

26. Ibid, p. 108.

27. Kant, *Anthropology*, p. 21.

28. Arendt, "Some Questions of Moral Philosophy," p. 81.

29. Ibid.

30. Ibid.; emphasis in original.

Chapter 3: Virginia Woolf and the Shadow of the "I"

Epigraph: Emmanuel Lévinas, *Difficult Freedom: Essays on Judaism*, trans. by Seán Hand (1990; repr., Baltimore: Johns Hopkins University Press, 1997), p. 100.

1. Virginia Woolf, *A Room of One's Own* (San Diego: Harcourt Brace Jovanovich, 1989).

2. Ibid., p. 99.

3. Ibid., pp. 99–100.

4. Ibid.

5. Ibid., p. 100.

6. Ibid.

7. Ibid., p. 102.

8. Ibid., p. 35.

9. Ibid., p. 74.

10. Ibid., p. 87.

11. Ibid.

12. Ibid., p. 74.

13. [Cavarero here refers to the derivation of these terms from the Latin *pendēre*, "to hang."—Trans.]

Chapter 4: Plato *Erectus Sed . . .*

Epigraph: Sigmund Freud, *Civilization and Its Discontents*, trans. James Strachey (New York: W. W. Norton, 1961), p. 54 n. 1.

1. Hans Blumenberg, *Höhlenausgänge* (Frankfurt am Main: Suhrkamp, 1989), 56. [All translations of Blumenberg are our own.—Trans.]

2. Luce Irigaray, *Speculum of the Other Woman*, trans. Gillian C. Gill (Ithaca, NY: Cornell University Press, 1985), pp. 243–44.

3. Blumenberg, *Höhlenausgänge*, 23.

4. Ibid., 25.

5. Ibid., 33.

6. Ibid., 34.

7. Umberto Curi, *La cognizione dell'amore: Eros e filosofia* (Milan: Feltrinelli, 1997), p. 73.

8. Plato, *Republic* 514a, trans. Allan Bloom, 2nd ed. (New York: Basic Books, 1968).

9. Ibid. 508c.

10. Ibid. 519d.

11. Ibid. 511c. On the complex question of the Orphic-Pythagorean influence on the myth of the cave, see Curi, *La cognizione dell'amore*, pp. 135–41.

12. Michel Foucault, *The Courage of Truth (the Government of Self and Others II): Lectures at the Collège de France, 1983–1984*, trans. Graham Burchell (New York: Palgrave Macmillan, 2011), p. 235.

13. Hannah Arendt, *The Human Condition* (Chicago: University of Chicago Press, 1958), p. 14.

14. Martin Heidegger, "Plato's Doctrine of Truth," trans. William McNeil, in *Pathmarks*, ed. William McNeil (Cambridge: Cambridge University Press, 1998), pp. 155–82.

15. Plato, *Cratylus* 384b, trans. Benjamin Jowett, in *The Collected Dialogues of Plato*, ed. Edith Hamilton and Huntington Cairns (New York: Pantheon, 1961).

16. Martin Heidegger, *The Essence of Truth: On Plato's Cave Allegory and Theaetetus*, trans. Ted Sadler (New York: Continuum, 2002), p. 68 n. 5.

17. For the concept of verticality within *orthos*, Franco Rendich, *Dizionario etimologico comparato delle lingue classiche indoeuropeo: Indoeuropeo, sanscrito, greco, latino* (Rome: Palombi, 2010). Here *orthos* is connected to the Latin *erectus*, via the common Sanskrit root *ir*, "to raise," "to get straight," "to move vertically."

18. Foucault, *Courage of the Truth*, pp. 218–19.

19. Ibid., p. 219.

20. See s.v. *orthos* in Pierre Chantraine, *Dictionnaire etymologique de la langue greque: Histoire des mots* (Paris: Klincksieck, 1968–80).

21. Plato, *Republic* 515c.

22. Plato, *Timaeus* 90a, trans. Benjamin Jowett, in *The Collected Dialogues of Plato*, ed. Edith Hamilton and Huntington Cairns (New York: Pantheon, 1961).

23. Ibid. 90b.

24. On this complex topic, see Stefano Salzani, "'Arbor Inversa': Studio

sulla tradizione simbolica dell'Albero Rovesciato," *Perennia Verba* 8–9 (2004–5): 152–97.

25. Aristotle, *Parts of Animals* 686a27–28, in *The Complete Works of Aristotle*, vol. 1, ed. Jonathan Barnes (Princeton, NJ: Princeton University Press, 1984).

Chapter 5: Men and Trees

Epigraph: Elizabeth Gaskell, *Ruth* (New York: Penguin, 1997), p. 345.

1. C. G. Jung, *Psychology and Alchemy*, trans. R. F. C. Hull (Princeton, NJ: Princeton University Press, 1968).

2. James Hillman, *The Soul's Code: In Search of Character and Calling* (New York: Random House / Warner Books, 1997), p. 279.

3. Ibid., p. 280.

4. See Stefano Salzani, "'Arbor Inversa': Studio sulla tradizione simbolica dell'Albero Rovesciato," *Perennia Verba* 8–9 (2004–5): 152–97.

5. Angelo Paciuchelli, *Lezioni morali sopra Giona profeta*, vol. 1 (Venice: Paolo Baglioni, 1664), p. 190. [Trans. by the translators of this volume.]

6. "Nothing entirely straight can be fashioned from the crooked wood of which humankind is made [Aus so krummem Holze, als woraus der Mensch gemacht ist, kann nichts ganz Gerades gezimmert werden]." See Immanuel Kant, "Idea for a Universal History from a Cosmopolitan Perspective," in *Toward Perpetual Peace and Other Writings on Politics, Peace, and History*, ed. Pauline Kleingeld, trans. David Colcasure (New Haven, CT: Yale University Press, 2006), p. 9.

7. Michel Foucault, *Discipline and Punish: The Birth of the Prison*, trans. Alan Sheridan (New York: Vintage, 1977), pp. 135–94.

8. [As Cavarero argues below, the Italian *torto* can mean not only "wrongdoing" or "injustice" but also "crooked" or "twisted." It is one of many terms (e.g., the English "tort") derived from the Latin *tortum* ('wrong" or "injustice'), which in turn is the substantive use of the Latin *tortus* ("twisted," "wrung," or "bent").—Trans.]

9. Lorenzo Bernini, *Apocalissi queer: Elementi di teoria antisociale* (Pisa: ETS, 2013), 25–26. [Trans. by the translators of this volume.]

10. Immanuel Kant, "The Metaphysics of Morals," in *Practical Philosophy*, ed. and trans. Mary Gregor (Cambridge: Cambridge University Press, 1996), pp. 426–27.

11. Ibid., p. 548.

12. Ibid., p. 549; emphasis in original.

13. Ibid.; emphasis in original.

Chapter 6: On Erect Posture

Epigraph: Arnold Gehlen, *Man: His Nature and Place in the World*, trans. Clare McMillan and Karl Pillemer (New York: Columbia University Press, 1988), p. 139.

1. Immanuel Kant, "Review of Moscati's Work *Of the Corporeal Essential Differences Between the Structure of Animals and Humans*," trans. Günter Zöller, in *Anthropology, History, and Education*, ed. Günter Zöller and Robert B. Louden (Cambridge: Cambridge University Press, 2007), pp. 79–81.

2. Pietro Moscati, *Delle corporee differenze essenziali che passano fra la struttura de' bruti e la umana: Discorso accademico letto nel teatro anatomico della Regia Università di Pavia* (Brescia: Rizzardi, 1770), p. 22. [Trans. by the translators of this volume.]

3. Ibid., p. 13. [Trans. by the translators of this volume.]

4. Ibid., pp. 19–20.

5. Kant, "Review of Moscati's Work," p. 79.

6. Immanuel Kant, "Of the Different Races of Human Beings," trans. Holly Wilson and Günter Zöller, in *Anthropology, History, Education*, pp. 84–97; "Universal Natural History and Theory of the Heavens or Essay on the Constitution and the Mechanical Origin of the Whole Universe According to Newtonian Principles," trans. Olaf Reinhardt, in *Natural Science*, ed. Eric Watkins (Cambridge: Cambridge University Press, 2012), pp. 182–308.

7. Kant, "Review of Moscati's Work," pp. 80–81; emphasis in original.

8. Ibid., p. 81.

9. Plato, *Statesman* 266b–267c, trans. J. B. Skemp, in *The Collected Dialogues of Plato*, ed. Edith Hamilton and Huntington Cairns (New York: Pantheon, 1961).

10. Johann Gottfried Herder, *On World History: An Anthology*, ed. Hans Adler and Ernest A. Menze, trans. Ernest A. Menze and Michael Palma (New York: Routledge, 1996), p. 135; emphasis in original, translation modified.

11. See, generally, Johann Gottfried Herder, *Outlines of a Philosophy of the History of Man*, trans. T. Churchill (London: Hanford, 1803).

12. Herder, *On World History*, p. 161.

13. Ibid., p. 129.

14. Kant, "Review of J. G. Herder's *Ideas for the Philosophy of the History of Humanity*," trans. Allen W. Wood, in *Anthropology, History, and Education*, p. 134.

15. Charles Darwin, *The Descent of Man and Selection in Relation to Sex: In Two Volumes* (New York: D. Appleton, 1872), p. 190.

16. Kant, "Review of J. G. Herder's *Ideas*," p. 127; emphasis in original.

17. Ibid.

18. Ibid., p. 133.

19. Ibid., p. 127.

20. Herder as quoted in Kant, "Review of J. G. Herder's *Ideas*," p. 127.

21. Ibid., p. 128.

22. Ibid.

23. Ibid.

24. Immanuel Kant, "Critique of Practical Reason," in *Practical Philosophy*, trans. Mary J. Gregor (Cambridge: Cambridge University press, 1996), p. 269; emphasis in original.

25. Ibid.

26. Ibid., p. 270; emphasis in original.

Chapter 7: Hobbes and the Macroanthropos

Epigraph: Peter Sloterdijk, *You Must Change Your Life*, trans. Wieland Hoban (Malden, MA: Polity, 2013), p. 12.

1. See Robert Pouchet, *La rectitudo chez saint Anselme: Un itinéraire augustinien de l'âme à Dieu* (Paris: Études Augustiniennes, 1964), p. 224. [Trans. by the translators of this volume.] This is a truly excellent and detailed work on the history of the category of *rectitudo* in the Christian tradition.

2. Ibid., p. 36. [Trans. by the translators of this volume.] See also Augustine, "On the Free Choice of the Will," in *On the Free Choice of the Will, On Grace and Free Choice, and Other Writings*, trans. Peter King (Cambridge: Cambridge University Press, 2010), bk. 3; Seneca, *Letters from a Stoic: Epistulae Morales ad Lucilium*, ed. and trans. Robin Campbell (New York: Penguin, 1969), pp. xv, 95, 57.

3. Hannah Arendt, *The Life of the Mind*, vol. 2 (New York: Harcourt Brace Jovanovich, 1978), p. 3.

4. Ibid., p. 84.

5. Thomas Aquinas, *Summa theologica*, vol. 19, ed. Thomas Gilby (Cambridge: Blackfriars; New York: McGraw-Hill, 1964–81), p. 71 (I-II, q. 26, a. 3).

6. Augustine, "On the Free Choice of the Will," in *On the Free Choice of the Will*, p. 74.

7. Thomas Hobbes, *On the Citizen*, ed. and trans. Richard Tuck and Michael Silverthorne (Cambridge: Cambridge University Press, 1998), p. 27.

8. Plato, *Republic* 368c–d.

9. Thomas Hobbes, *Leviathan*, ed. Richard Tuck (Cambridge: Cambridge University Press, 1996), p. 9.

10. Ibid., p. 70.

11. Hobbes, *On the Citizen*, p. 27.

12. Ibid., p. 26.

13. Hobbes, *Leviathan*, p. 90.

Chapter 8: Upright Before the Dead
Epigraph: Ernst Jünger, *Der Gordische Knoten* (Frankfurt am Main: Klostermann, 1953).

1. Elias Canetti, "Power and Survival," in *The Conscience of Words*, trans. Joachim Neugroschel (New York: Seabury, 1979), p. 16.

2. Elias Canetti, *Crowds and Power*, trans. Carol Stewart (New York: Viking, 1962), p. 227.

3. Canetti, "Power and Survival," p. 15.

4. Ibid., p. 15.

5. Ibid., pp. 19–20.

6. Canetti, *Crowds and Power*, p. 227.

7. Canetti, "Power and Survival," p. 15.

8. Ibid., p. 17.

9. Ibid., p. 21.

10. Ibid., p. 15.

11. Canetti, *Crowds and Power*, p. 387.

12. Ibid.; emphasis in original.

13. Ibid., pp. 387–88.

14. Ibid., p. 389.

Chapter 9: The *Allegory of Inclination*
Epigraph: Susan Vreeland, *The Passion of Artemisia* (New York: Penguin, 2002), p. 87.

1. Dante, *Inferno* V.39, trans. Robert and Jean Hollander (New York: Anchor, 2000), pp. 92–93.

2. Plato, *Republic* 501c, trans. Allan Bloom, 2nd ed. (New York: Basic Books, 1968); translation modified.

3. For an exhaustive treatment of this theme, see Don Fowler, *Lucretius on Atomic Motion: A Commentary on De Rerum Natura* (Oxford: Oxford University Press, 2002), esp. pp. 301ff.

4. Lucretius, *De rerum natura libri sex*, trans. H. A. J. Munro (Cambridge: Deighton, Bell, 1866), p. 33.

5. Jacques Derrida, "My Chances / *Mes chances*," in *Psyche: Inventions of the Other*, vol. 1, ed. Peggy Kamuf and Elizabeth Rottenberg (Stanford, CA: Stanford University Press, 2007), pp. 350–51.

Chapter 10: Leonardo and Maternal Inclination
Epigraph: Ramón Eder, *La vida ondulante* (Seville: Renacimiento, 2012).

1. See Luisa Accati, *Il mostro e la bella: Padre e madre nell'educazione cattolica dei sentimenti*, ed. Raffaello Cortina (Milan: Cortina, 1998), pp. 82–113

and 163–202. Besides offering a well-documented analysis of the Marian tradition, the book also critically revisits the stereotype of maternity around the figure of the Madonna.

2. Hannah Arendt, "Some Questions of Moral Philosophy," in *Responsibility and Judgment*, ed. Jerome Kohn (New York: Schocken, 2003), p. 81.

3. Ibid., pp. 116, 142.

4. Judith Butler, *Giving an Account of Oneself: A Critique of Ethical Violence* (New York: Fordham University Press, 2005), p. 110.

5. Hannah Arendt, *The Human Condition* (Chicago: University of Chicago Press, 1958), pp. 176–77.

6. See Roberto Esposito, *Immunitas: The Protection and Negation of Life*, trans. Zakiya Hanafi (Cambridge: Polity, 2011).

7. Carol Gilligan, *In a Different Voice: Psychological Theory and Women's Development* (Cambridge, MA: Harvard University Press, 1982).

8. For an extended discussion of defenselessness and vulnerability, see my *Horrorism: Naming Contemporary Violence*, trans. William McCuaig (New York: Columbia University Press, 2009).

9. In *Elements of Law, Natural and Politic* (2.IV.3), *De cive* (IX.2) and *Leviathan* (XX.5), Hobbes maintains that the maternal entitlement to the child does not depend on procreation but on the capability to save or kill it. See my *Horrorism* (pp. 22–26) for a discussion on the essential elements of this ethical problem.

10. Arendt, "Some Questions of Moral Philosophy," p. 51.

11. On the maternal as central figure for the rethinking of ontology and politics, see Olivia Guaraldo, *Comunità e vulnerabilità: Per una critica politica della violenza* (Pisa: ETS, 2012), pp. 58–59.

12. See Accati, *Il mostro e la bella*, p. 89. [Trans. by the translators of this volume.]

Chapter 11: "A Child Has Been Born unto Us"

Epigraph: Francesca Rigotti, *Partorire con il corpo e con la mente: Creatività, filosofia, maternità* (Turin: Bollati Boringhieri, 2010).

1. Hannah Arendt, *The Human Condition* (Chicago: University of Chicago Press, 1958), pp. 246–47.

2. Ibid., p. 247.

3. For an insight into this complex issue, see Susan Young-Ah Gottlieb, *Regions of Sorrow: Anxiety and Messianism in Hannah Arendt and W. H. Auden* (Stanford, CA: Stanford University Press, 2003), pp. 136ff.

4. Arendt, *Human Condition*, p. 7.

5. Augustine, *The City of God Against the Pagans*, ed. and trans. R. W.

Dyson (Cambridge: Cambridge University Press, 1998), p. 532 (XII.21). [In *The Human Condition*, where Arendt incorrectly attributes this passage to chapter 20 of book XII of *De civitate Dei*, she translates the phrase "that there be a beginning, man was created before whom there was nobody" (177). R. W. Dyson, by contrast, translates the phrase, "in order that there might be this beginning, therefore, a man was created before whom no man existed."—Trans.]

6. Hannah Arendt, *The Origins of Totalitarianism* (Harcourt Brace Jovanovich, 1973), p. 479.

7. Arendt, *Human Condition*, p. 9.

8. Hannah Arendt, "Introduction into Politics," in *The Promise of Politics*, ed. Jerome Kohn (New York: Schocken, 2005), p. 96.

9. Ibid., p. 177.

10. Ibid., pp. 176–77.

11. Ibid., p. 176; emphasis in original.

12. Ibid.

13. Ibid., p. 246.

14. Ibid.

15. Hannah Arendt, *The Life of the Mind*, vol. 1 (New York: Harcourt Brace, 1978), p. 80.

16. Arendt, *Human Condition*, p. 247.

17. See Bonnie Honig, *Emergency Politics: Paradox, Law, Democracy* (Princeton, NJ: Princeton University Press, 2009), pp. 92–93. Honig offers a political inquiry into the theme of the miracle, proposing a thought-provoking comparison between Rosenzweig and Arendt.

18. Simona Forti, *Hannah Arendt tra filosofia e politica* (Milan: Bruno Mondadori, 2006), p. 268.

19. Miguel Vatter, "Natality and Biopolitics in Hannah Arendt," *Revista de Ciencia Política* 26:2 (2006): 145.

20. See, above all, Giorgio Agamben, *Homo Sacer: Sovereign Power and Bare Life*, trans. Daniel Heller-Roazen (Stanford, CA: Stanford University Press, 1998), 1–14; Simona Forti, *New Demons: Rethinking Power and Evil Today*, trans. Zakiya Hanafi (Stanford, CA: Stanford University Press, 2014), pp. 125–82.

21. Arendt, *Origins of Totalitarianism*, p. 455.

22. Vatter, "Natality and Biopolitics," p. 157.

23. Arendt, *Human Condition*, p. 9.

24. Ibid., p. 247.

25. Ibid., p. 7.

26. See Paul Kottman, *A Politics of the Scene* (Stanford, CA: Stanford University Press, 2008), especially the chapter entitled "Toward a Politics of the Scene."

27. Arendt, *Human Condition*, pp. 198–99.

28. Peg Birmingham, *Hannah Arendt and Human Rights* (Bloomington: Indiana University Press), p. 85. This book presents a broad and demanding interpretation of the Arendtian concept of natality, and also testifies the growing interest on this topic. Besides the already mentioned essay by Miguel Vatter, see also Patricia Bowen- Moore, *Hannah Arendt's Philosophy of Natality* (New York: St. Martin's, 1989); Margaret Durst, "On the Concept of Birth in Hannah Arendt," *Phenomenological Inquiry* 25 (2001): 72–84; and Anne O'Byrne, *Natality and Finitude* (Bloomington: Indiana University Press, 2010), esp. chap. 4.

29. Arendt, *Human Condition*, p. 177.

30. Ibid., p. 8; emphasis in original, text modified.

31. Ibid.

32. Ibid.

33. John Locke, *Two Treatises of Government and A Letter Concerning Toleration*, ed. Ian Shapiro (New Haven, CT: Yale University Press, 2003), p. 123.

34. See Charles Taylor, *Sources of the Self: The Making of the Modern Identity* (Cambridge: Cambridge University Press, 1989), p. 160.

Chapter 12: Schemata for a Postural Ethics

Epigraph: Susan Hill, *The Woman in Black: A Ghost Story* (New York: Vintage, 2011), p. 11.

1. Hobbes identified the power of the mother over the infant with the power of destruction. See Thomas Hobbes, *The Elements of Law, Natural and Politic: Part I, Human Nature; Part II, De Corpore Politico* (Oxford: Oxford University Press, 1994), chap. 23 (pt. 2, chap. 4, § 3), pp. 130–31.

2. Julia Kristeva, *Melanie Klein*, trans. Ross Guberman (New York: Columbia University Press, 2001), p. 155.

3. Angela Putino, *Amiche mie isteriche* (Naples: Cronopio, 1998), p. 60. [Trans. by the translators of this volume.]

4. This book has generated a wide critical response. See, for instance, *An Ethics of Care: Feminist and Interdisciplinary Perspectives*, ed. Mary Jeanne Larrabee (New York: Routledge, 1993); Virginia Held, *The Ethics of Care: Personal, Political, Global* (Oxford: Oxford University Press, 2006); and Elena Pulcini, *La cura del mondo: Paura e responsabilità nell'età globale* (Turin: Bollati Boringhieri, 2009).

5. Pulcini, *La cura del mondo*, p. 252.

6. See the important analysis by Joan C. Tronto, *Moral Boundaries: A Political Argument for an Ethic of Care* (New York: Routledge, 1993).

7. Held, *Ethics of Care*, p. 78.

8. Eva Feder Kittay, *Love's Labor: Essays on Equality, Dependency, and Care* (New York: Routledge, 1999), p. 92.

9. Alasdair C. MacIntyre, *Dependent Rational Animals: Why Human Beings Need the Virtues* (Chicago: Open Court, 1999).

10. Ibid., p. 74.

11. Ibid., p. 104.

12. Hans Jonas, *The Imperative of Responsibility*, trans. Hans Jonas with David Herr (Chicago: University of Chicago Press, 1984), p. 134.

13. Ibid.

14. Ibid., p. 131.

15. Ibid., p. 135.

16. Such is the title of Sara Ruddick's successful book *Maternal Thinking: Toward a Politics of Peace* (London: The Women Press, 1989). See also Francesca Rigotti, *Partorire con il corpo e con la mente* (Turin: Bollati Boringhieri 2010), esp. pp. 55–69.

17. See Arnold Gehlen, *Man: His Nature and Place in the World*, trans. Clare McMillan and Karl Pillemer (New York: Columbia University Press, 1988), p. 150.

18. Judith Butler, *Precarious Life: The Powers of Mourning and Violence* (London: Verso, 2004), p. 41.

19. See Hans Kelsen, *Essays in Legal and Moral Philosophy*, trans. Peter Heath (Dordrecht: Reidel, 1974), p. 106.

20. Ibid.

Coda

1. Jacques Derrida, *Adieu to Emmanuel Levinas*, trans. Pascale-Anne Brault and Michael Naas (Stanford, CA: Stanford University Press, 1999), p. 2: translation modified.

2. Emmanuel Lévinas, *Entre Nous: Thinking-of-the-Other*, trans. Michael B. Smith and Barbara Harshav (London: Continuum, 2006), pp. 144, 111. Cf. Derrida, *Adieu*, p. 121.

3. Emmanuel Lévinas, *Proper Names*, trans. Michael B. Smith (Stanford, CA: Stanford University Press, 1996), pp. 73–74.

4. Emmanuel Lévinas, *Otherwise Than Being, or Beyond Essence*, trans. Alphonso Lingis (Pittsburgh: Duquesne University Press, 1998), p. 105; translation modified.

5. Emmanuel Lévinas, "Transcendence and Intelligibility," in *Emmanuel Lévinas: Basic Philosophical Writings*, ed. Adrian Theodor Peperzak, Simon Critcheley, and Robert Bernasconi (Bloomington: Indiana University Press 1996), p. 151; emphasis in original.

6. Emmanuel Lévinas, *Time and the Other*, trans. Richard A. Cohen (Pittsburgh: Duquesne University Press, 1987), p. 98.

7. Emmanuel Lévinas, *Totality and Infinity: An Essay on Exteriority*, trans. Alphonso Lingis (Pittsburgh: Duquesne University Press, 1969), p. 44.

8. Kathleen Freeman, *Ancilla to the Pre-Socratic Philosophers* (Cambridge, MA: Harvard University Press, 1996), 43.

9. Emmanuel Lévinas, "Is Ontology Fundamental?" in *Emmanuel Lévinas: Basic Philosophical Writings*, p. 2.

10. Lévinas, *Proper Names*, p. 81.

11. See the preface to the very useful collection *Emmanuel Lévinas: Basic Philosophical Writings*, p. xi.

12. Lévinas, *Totality and Infinity*, pp. 123–24; translation modified.

13. Emmanuel Lévinas, *Humanism of the Other*, trans. Nidra Poller (Urbana: University of Illinois Press, 2003), p. 35; emphasis in original, translation modified.

14. Lévinas, *Totality and Infinity*, p. 80.

15. Lévinas, *Humanism of the Other*, p. 29.

16. Lévinas, *Proper Names*, p. 93; translation modified.

17. Plato, *Republic* 509b, trans. Allan Bloom, 2nd ed. (New York: Basic Books, 1968).

18. Lévinas, *Totality and Infinity*, p. 103.

19. Ibid., p. 200.

20. Lévinas, *Humanism of the Other*, p. 54.

21. Lévinas, *Time and the Other*, p. 42.

22. Lévinas, *Totality and Infinity*, p. 79.

23. Lévinas, *Proper Names*, p. 110

24. Lévinas, *Totality and Infinity*, pp. 139, 135; translation modified.

25. Ibid., pp. 137–38; emphasis in original.

26. Ibid., p. 117; emphasis in original.

27. Ibid., p. 77.

28. Lévinas, "Transcendence and Height," in *Emmanuel Lévinas: Basic Philosophical Writings*, p. 25.

29. Emmanuel Lévinas, "Judaism and Kenosis," in *In the Time of the Nations*, trans. Michael B. Smith (Bloomington: Indiana University Press, 1994), p. 115. In passing, the reader should note the figure of a God who is bent over, even if Lévinas does not relate it to the theme of inclination but to humility.

30. Lévinas, *Totality and Infinity*, p. 34.

31. Jacques Derrida, "Violence and Metaphysics," in *Writing and Difference*, trans. Alan Bass (Chicago: University of Chicago Press, 1978), pp. 108–9.

32. Lévinas, *Humanism of the Other*, p. 36.

33. Lévinas, *Totality and Infinity*, p. 144.

34. Ibid., p. 134.

35. Ibid., p. 141.

36. Ibid., p. 118; emphasis in original.

37. Ibid., p. 144.

38. Ibid., p. 147; emphasis in original.

39. Derrida, *Adieu*, p. 44.

40. Lévinas, *Totality and Infinity*, p. 117.

41. Ibid.

42. Ibid., p. 149.

43. Ibid., p. 160.

44. Ibid., p. 117; translation modified.

45. Ibid., p. 152.

46. Ibid., p. 159; emphasis in original.

47. Ibid., p. 156.

48. Ibid., p. 155; emphasis in original.

49. Ibid.

50. Lévinas, "Transcendence and Height," in *Emmanuel Lévinas: Basic Philosophical Writings*, p. 14.

51. Lévinas, *Existence and Existents*, trans. Alphonso Lingis (The Hague: Nijhoff, 1978), p. 100.

52. Derrida, "Violence and Metaphysics," p. 320 n. 92.

53. Lévinas, *Totality and Infinity*, p. 257.

54. Ibid., p. 259.

55. Ibid., pp. 260, 263.

56. Ibid., p. 259.

57. Ibid., p. 277; emphasis in original.

58. Ibid., p. 282.

59. Lévinas, *Proper Names*, p. 73.

60. Lévinas, *Otherwise Than Being*, p. 88.

61. Ibid., p. 58.

62. Lévinas, *Proper Names*, p. 73.

63. Lévinas, *Entre Nous*, p. 177.

64. Lévinas, *Otherwise Than Being*, p. 56.

65. Lévinas, *Entre Nous*, p. 58.

66. Ibid., p. 59.

67. Ibid., p. 58.

68. Lévinas, *Otherwise Than Being*, p. 91.

69. Numbers 11:12–13 (RSV).

70. Lévinas, *Otherwise Than Being*, pp. 75–76.

71. Ibid., pp. 76.

72. Ibid., pp. 78–79.

73. Ibid., p. 76.

74. Ibid.

75. Ibid., p. 79.

76. Ibid., p. 80; translation modified. [In Silvo Petrosino's 1983 Italian translation of *Autrement qu'être*, from which Cavarero quotes here, this phrase is italicized. It also is italicized in the French original. Not so the English translation. For the purposes of conveying Cavarero's argument, we have italicized it here.—Trans.]

77. Lisa Guenther, *The Gift of the Other: Levinas and the Politics of Reproduction* (Albany: State University of New York Press, 2006), p. 100.

78. Ibid., p. 6.

79. Lévinas, *Totality and Infinity*, p. 34.

80. Lévinas, *Proper Names*, p. 27.

81. Ibid., p. 32.

82. Lévinas, *Ethics and Infinity*, p. 98; emphasis in original

83. Lévinas, *Otherwise Than Being*, p. 192 n. 29.

84. Lévinas, *Entre Nous*, p. 125.

85. Ibid., p. 128.

86. Among the many difficulties the Lévinasian lexicon poses, there is the positive and nonconformist use of the term *metaphysics*, which some of his contemporaries use to designate what he calls "ontology." By warning in *Totality and Infinity* that the concept of metaphysics "has an entirely different meaning" (302), the philosopher prepares the readers to understand it as a synonym of transcendence, as a relation to infinity that happens in the encounter with the face of the other. Pre-originary and an-archic, metaphysics, or better, the metaphysics of ethics, is therefore anterior to ontology.

87. Emmanuel Lévinas, "From Ethics to Exegesis," in *In the Time of the Nations*, p. 111.

88. Emmanuel Lévinas, *Difficult Freedom: Essays on Judaism*, trans. Seán Hand (Baltimore: Johns Hopkins University Press, 1990), p. 8.

89. Lévinas, *Totality and Infinity*, p. 80; emphasis in original.

90. Lévinas, *Proper Names*, p. 32; emphasis in original.

91. See Francesca Consolaro, "Il 'vulnerabile' come chiave del 'mondo che viene': Considerazioni etimologiche," *Filosofia Politica* 1 (2009): 45–46.

92. Lévinas, *Totality and Infinity*, pp. 257–58.

93. Emmanuel Lévinas, "Peace and Proximity," in *Alterity and Transcendence*, trans. Michael B. Smith (London: Athlone, 1999), pp. 139–41; cf. Lévinas, *Entre Nous*, 161.

94. Derrida, *Adieu*, p. 3.

95. Emmanuel Lévinas, "The Other in Proust," in *The Lévinas Reader*, ed. Seán Hand (Oxford: Blackwell, 1989), p. 164.

96. Lévinas, *Otherwise Than Being*, 77.

97. Lévinas, *Humanism of the Other*, p. 55.

98. Lévinas, "Diachrony and Representation," in *Time and the Other*, p. 107; emphasis in original.

99. Lévinas, "Peace and Proximity," p. 135.

100. Judith Butler, *Giving an Account of Oneself* (New York: Fordham University Press, 2005), p. 90; emphasis in original.

101. Lévinas, "Meaning and Sense," in *Emmanuel Lévinas: Basic Writings*, p. 53.

102. [Cavarero translates *Befindlichkeit* as "la paura per altri" or "fear for others." In English the term hasn't found a stable translation and has been rendered alternately as "state-of-mind" (by John Macquarrie and Edward Robinson), as "already-having-found-oneself-there-ness" (by William Richardson), and as "disposedness" (by Theodore Kisiel). Whereas certain authoritative sources (e.g. the *Stanford Encyclopedia of Philosophy*) lean toward Kisiel's translation, still others prefer "situatedness." Insofar as *Befindlichkeit* indicates a condition for "moods," which is more in line with Cavarero's inquiry into "inclinations," we have here opted to translate *Befindlichkeit* as "affectivity."—Trans.]

103. Lévinas, *Entre Nous*, p. 100.

104. Lévinas, *Ethics and Infinity*, pp. 99–100; translation modified.

105. Ibid., p. 99.

106. Lévinas, "Diachrony and Representation," in *Time and the Other*, p. 110.

107. Lévinas, *Ethics and Infinity*, p. 95.

108. Ibid., p. 100.

109. Ibid.

110. Derrida, *Adieu*, p. 56.

111. Francesco Paolo Ciglia, *Un passo fuori dall'uomo: La genesi del pensiero di Lévinas* (Padova: CEDAM, 1988), p. 204. [Trans. by the translators of this volume.]

112. Lévinas, *Ethics and Infinity*, p. 89.

113. Ibid., p. 95.

114. Ibid., p. 90.

115. Ibid., pp. 80–81.

116. Lévinas, "Peace and Proximity," p. 144.

117. Lévinas, *Ethics and Infinity*, p. 80; emphasis in original.

118. Lévinas, "Peace and Proximity," p. 136.

SQUARE ONE
First-Order Questions in the Humanities

PAUL A. KOTTMAN, Series Editor

This series reclaims the authority of humanistic inquiry for a broad, educated readership by tackling questions of common concern, such as: 'What do we value and why?' 'To what kind of life can we aspire, given the contours of modern society?' 'What is it to lead a free life?' 'What is the place of the imagination in our society?' 'Why do, or why should, we still care about particular artworks?' Square One shows how questions like these are reflected in our philosophy, art, literature, politics, and ethics.

Pushing beyond the twin trends that have come to characterize much academic writing in the humanities—increasing specialization, on the one hand, and interdisciplinary 'crossings' on the other—Square One cuts across and through fields in order to show the relevance and importance of humanistic inquiry for an intellectual readership. Series books are therefore meant to be accessible and compelling to educated non-specialists as well as academic experts. Rather than address only a particular academic group of experts, or simply open new, interdisciplinary terrain from within traditional fields, they focus on a first-order question in topics with clear relevance to traditional domains of humanistic inquiry.

The authorized representative in the EU for product safety and compliance is:
Mare Nostrum Group
B.V Doelen 72
4831 GR Breda
The Netherlands

www.ingramcontent.com/pod-product-compliance
Lightning Source LLC
Chambersburg PA
CBHW050442290526
45786CB00006B/2133